New Possibilities
for
Small Churches

School of Divinity

Gardner-Webb University
School of Divinity

New Possibilities
for
Small Churches

Edited by
Douglas Alan Walrath

The Pilgrim Press
New York

The biblical quotations are from the *Revised Standard Version of the Bible,* copyright 1946, 1952 and © 1971 by the Division of Christian Education, National Council of Churches, and are used by permission.

Library of Congress Cataloging in Publication Data
Main entry under title:

New possibilities for small churches.

Includes bibliographical references.
Contents: Introduction / Douglas Alan Walrath—
Possibilities for small churches today / Douglas Alan
Walrath—Worship in the small congregation / Paul
Gibson—[etc.]
1. Small churches—Addresses, essays, lectures.
I. Walrath, Douglas Alan, 1933–
BV637.8.N48   1983   254   83-6252
ISBN 0-8298-0668-7

The Pilgrim Press, 132 West 31 Street, New York, NY 10001

Contributors

CARL S. DUDLEY *(United Presbyterian Church)* is professor of church and community at McCormick Theological Seminary, Chicago, Illinois. He also consults regularly with various church groups. His work covers a wide range of subjects, including help for small congregations.

THEODORE H. ERICKSON *(United Church of Christ)* currently carries responsibility in the area of mission strategy for the United Church Board for Homeland Ministries. His innovative work with small churches stretches over more than two decades.

PAUL GIBSON *(Anglican Church in Canada)* currently serves as liturgical officer for his denomination. Formerly, he was responsible for continuing education programs for clergy.

LYNNE JOSSELYN *(United Methodist Church)* is the district superintendent for the Southern District, Maine Conference. Prior to her present appointment, she served as a pastor of small congregations in that conference.

EMMANUEL L. McCALL *(Southern Baptist Convention)* is his denomination's Home Mission Board executive for black church relations. He is well regarded as an interpreter of the minority church to the majority church.

LOREN B. MEAD *(Episcopal Church)* serves as executive director of the Alban Institute in Washington, DC. The institute provides a variety of consultant services and resources to all levels of the church.

DOUGLAS ALAN WALRATH *(Reformed Church in America)* divides his time among consulting, teaching at Bangor Theological Seminary, writing, and operating a small farm in Strong, Maine. Formerly, he served as a local pastor and church executive.

Contents

Introduction

Leading the Small Church:
The State of the Art Today

PROBABLY THE MOST significant development in the ecclesiastical world in the past decade is the unabashed
affirmation of the small church. While it is difficult to discover where this movement began, it clearly gathered
momentum from the Hartford Seminary-sponsored sym-
posium on the small church, held in January 1976. A working group of leaders presented papers that probed the history, sociology, organization, leadership, program, image,
and expectations of small congregations. The insights and
suggestions contained in these papers were processed by
more than two hundred participating leaders from small congregations and all levels of a dozen denominations. The resulting book carries the provocative title *Small Churches
Are Beautiful!*[1]

Today many church leaders are soberer than that title
implies, but they are still eager to affirm the place of the
small church now and in the future. See, for example, *Small
Churches Are the Right Size* by David R. Ray.[2] Small
churches are rarely described as being obsolete or dispensable anymore. Few advocate the merging of small churches
into larger organizations as a probable outcome for all or
even most small congregations. Such talk was common as
recently as a decade ago.

Now it is known that the small congregation is not only hardy, but resistant to that kind of change—legitimately resistant. Also, it has been discovered that a small church meets needs and has ministry possibilities a large church does not. Some church members cannot cope with a large church and do not want to belong to one. A small church meets their psychological, cultural, and religious needs more effectively. One of the major reasons such persons participate in a small church is because it is small. I am surprised how long it took many of us to understand this reality.

But what does small mean? Perhaps the most elusive problem of the small church is defining a small church. I worked hard at this problem in my 1980 study of small congregations. Under the auspices of the Program Committee for Professional Church Leadership of the National Council of Churches, I studied the manner in which major denominations in the United States and Canada support leaders in "small" congregations. I found most define small with a number, with no small amount of disagreement among them (and sometimes within them) about the number of members below which a congregation should be considered small.

Today if one were seeking to define a small congregation by number of members, one would find opinions ranging from one hundred to three hundred fifty members. The precise measure depends, to some degree, on how a denomination counts its members (confirmed only or baptized? actives only or all those enrolled?). The difficulty I find in most attempts to characterize a small congregation with a number is not in disagreement over which number is the correct number. In the end, nothing significant about the congregation seems to be concluded by employing a number. Usually, a working definition is framed and this, not the number, is what is used.

For example, small means marginal—unable to survive

alone economically, to carry on certain programs, or to employ full-time pastoral leadership. Small means a congregation that needs help from beyond itself, either from denominational sources or by linking with other congregations.

The small church can also be characterized in terms of organizational dynamics. The best of these characterizations, in my opinion, is offered by Carl Dudley. He defines the small church as a single cell with a single center. Everyone can know about everyone else.[3] This definition feels most satisfying when I apply it to the small church where I am a member. I rarely think about how many of us members there are, but when we gather I am conscious of who is present and who is not.

Probably defining the small church is a function of purpose, and no single definition serves all purposes. In a world of rising institutional costs, small means marginal, unable to make it alone institutionally in one or more respects. Small also means a certain quality of life, a group where people know about one another and where relationships matter more than program.

For those who lead small congregations or work with persons who do, *all* the definitions are important, because at some point they will probably have to cope with the realities to which each definition points. A person who likes a small congregation has to be able to work with its marginality *and* be comfortable in a group where everybody knows (and remembers) about everybody else—including all about the leader.

The contributors to this book view the small congregation with a variety of definitions in mind. The result is a variety of insight that will be helpful to the leaders of small congregations—lay and clergy, local and denominational. Each chapter offers each category of leader some suggestions that can be employed directly. Suggestions more useful to one category of leader are also important for the others to know about. Originally, the substance of each chapter was presented to those gathered for a consultation on Leadership Issues in Small Congregations sponsored by the Program Committee for Professional Church Leadership of the National Council of Churches, in March 1981. One hundred sixty-five small-church leaders heard and discussed the presentations. Their responses and suggestions have been incorporated at many points.

In the opening chapter I offer an overview of the environments or social contexts that surround small congregations today. I believe that the near-devastating effects of social change on small congregations are underestimated by most local and denominational leaders. Many small congregations are not only small; they are significantly smaller. That dimension gives an uncomfortable bite to their small experience. They feel out of step with society as a whole; they live in subcultures at odds with the direction mainstream U.S. culture (and denominations) has taken in the past several decades. Bigger is better, management by objectives, ministers as professionals, and church growth are of another world. Those who would be helpers in and to small congregations need to find a style of helping that is suitable to the church as well as the times.

In chapter 2 Paul Gibson, of the Anglican Church in Canada, turns to the difficult but critical issue of worship in the small church. With the exception of William H. Willimon and Robert L. Wilson's book, *Preaching and Worship in the Small Church*, surprisingly little has been written in this area.[4] Gibson shows clearly that, at its roots, Christian worship is a small-scale experience; both the synagogue and the upper room involved small groups. He offers sound principles that leaders in small congregations can employ as they build their worship life. He draws us away from the norm of worship as a performance and into the experience of participating in worship, encourages a group planning effort for the small congregation's worship, and suggests help that judicatories can offer the small congregation to enhance its worship.

The next three chapters deal with pastoring. In the first of these chapters Carl Dudley offers ten characteristics of small congregations that establish "perimeters for constructive pastoral leadership." Small congregations have a strong people-concern, live on people-time, are carriers of history, trust face-to-face information, and so on.

Dudley helps us feel the life of the small church as well as understand it. Above all, he tells us the small church wants a pastor who is a lover, one who will venture "beyond the safety of organizational props into the uncertainties of walking with people who need God's help."

Emmanuel L. McCall, director of Black Church Relations for the Southern Baptist Convention, describes the unique opportunities and problems of the ethnic/minority small-church pastor. Unique opportunities include the assumption on the part of the congregation that the pastor will extend his or her priestly function beyond the congregation into the larger community, acting as an advocate. Problems include the near-necessity of being bivocational—often with a second occupation that is of low stature in the eyes of the community—educational limitations, and the majority community's lack of appreciation of his or her and the congregation's needs.

Lynne Josselyn helps us understand the support needed by women who minister to small congregations. She tells of her own difficult journey into ministry, one carried through virtually without any support. She argues convincingly that the church must build a support *system* to help women become effective ministers. She describes the natural gifts women bring to ministry.

Chapters by Loren Mead and Theodore Erickson address important organizational attitudes with which small-church leaders—lay as well as pastors—must cope. Loren Mead suggests interventions by judicatory representatives that can be helpful to small congregations. He begins by showing why small congregations need to share in setting the agenda and style of interventions by their judicatory. For example, they need to ask whose interests will be served by the intervention: the judicatory's alone or the judicatory's *and* the congregation's? Mead details some often uncomfortable questions that need to be considered by both judicatory leaders and pastors as they plan to work together. He shares patterns of judicatory staffing that lead to a more effective resource system for aiding small congregations and outlines key change points where judicatory intervention in a small congregation is likely to be most helpful.

Theodore Erickson tackles the difficult issue of small churches' typical feelings of powerlessness. Drawing on his experience in the well-known United Church Small Church Project (of which he was the prime architect), he explains how small churches can move toward empowerment by developing an effective leadership structure. He outlines the key role an intervening agent or consultant plays in the empowerment process and offers as an example one region from the small-church project where theory has been translated into actual empowerment of small congregations.

Despite its multiple authorship this book offers a variety of integrated suggestions to those who live and work in small congregations. It begins with a clarification of the social and organizational context of the small church, moves to issues and suggestions of special concern to pastors, and concludes with an examination of organizational issues of concern to both lay and judicatory leaders and to pastors. Along the way one discovers that (to use Loren Mead's words) "while small is *not* always beautiful, it is enough . . . for keeping on, . . . for faithfulness, . . . for holding lives and families together, . . . for making a contribution to a community, . . . for praying, for following Jesus. What else do we need?"

A few personal words of appreciation are in order.

The Leadership Issues in Small Congregations project of the National Council of Churches would not have come into being without the vision of Professional Church Leadership executive James W. Gunn. He has provided constant support throughout the project and was the first to suggest that the papers presented to the Detroit Consultation be gathered into a book. I have come to respect him as a colleague and to enjoy his friendship.

Marion M. Meyer of The Pilgrim Press has provided the editorial encouragement that made early publication of this book possible.

My wife, Sherry, served as registrar and hostess to the 170 participants of the Detroit Consultation. In the months since, through many hours of writing and rewriting, she has been both gracious and graceful. I am grateful.

Douglas Alan Walrath
Strong, Maine

New Possibilities
for
Small Churches

1

Possibilities for Small Churches Today

Douglas Alan Walrath

THE TRAIT I appreciate most about my Maine neighbors is their blunt simplicity. They have a way of quickly going to the heart of the matter—whatever the matter is.

Not long ago my truck was running poorly, so I made an appointment to take it to the garage. When I drove it in I took some pains to explain to the mechanic what appeared, to me, to be the cause of the truck's peculiar behavior. He listened with active disinterest.

Several hours later I called to check on the mechanic's progress. The service manager answered, and we had the following Maine-style conversation.

"How's my truck?" I asked.

"Runs fine," he replied. Silence.

"What did Kim (the mechanic) do to it?" I asked, in an attempt to stretch out the conversation.

"He fixed it!" was the impatient reply. More silence.

"Thanks, I'll be over to get it," was how I struggled out of the silence.

After I paid my bill (it was marked "labor—$6.00") I took

the truck for a test drive. He was right. It ran beautifully. In fact, I was so pleased I stopped back at the garage to congratulate the mechanic.

"Thanks for taking care of the problem with my truck; it certainly does run fine."

"You're welcome," he replied. As I turned to leave he added, "It wasn't what you thought it was!"

I suppose I deserved that response for trying to tell him how to do his work. I have been similarly chagrined and even more frustrated at times in the course of my work with small churches over the past two decades. All too often, even when I am certain I know what is wrong, someone in the local church will show me how my insight is lacking.

As a result of sharing my frustration with others who work with small churches I have found a common experience: No one inside or beyond the congregation has the needed insight. Not only does the church not run fine, it does not run at all anymore. Even though we as leaders put forth our best efforts to help, the congregations still slip away, and we ache to know why.

Change—It Is Bigger Than All of Us

After years of frustration it has become apparent to me that the real causes of the painful problems besetting small congregations will *not* be discovered by searching inside. The causes are beyond inside. Most of them originate outside the church.

This insight did not come easy, yet in retrospect I believe it is worth all the struggle that was necessary to clarify it. It is the key discovery. When looking inside the church for the causes, the tendency is to look for someone to blame for the problems. Only as all of us give up blaming one another for the current adversities of small congregations does attention shift to the more productive search for causes rather than scapegoats. Let me illustrate the point with two incidents out of my own discovery of the powerful effects social change has on congregations.

I completed seminary in the church boom time of the mid-1950s. Like many clergy of the time, I congratulated myself as hordes of young couples and children swarmed into church and Sunday school. What a good job we were all doing! A dozen years later, in most places, the gains had turned to losses. I moved up from a small congregation to a large congregation, hoping the move would bring better results from my ministry. It did not. I discovered that one can lose more members faster in a large church than in a small one, because there are so many more to lose. The church board was quite clear about the problem: It was me. I knew otherwise; I was trying harder than I had ten years earlier, and with a decade of experience I was more capable than I had been in the boom times. But even my greater capability could not counter the overwhelming effects of social change. We were in a new time.

In trying to cope I decided, among other courses of action, to seek a new perspective on the church, one that was different from that which I had been given in seminary. I enrolled in graduate school at a nearby university to pursue an advanced degree in sociology. To fulfill the requirements for one of my first research courses, I interviewed members of a large, suburban congregation. Given my theological orientation and my experience as a pastor, my questions, quite naturally, focused on such factors as the appeal of the local minister and the effectiveness of that particular congregation's program. Only at my professor's insistence did I add social and demographic questions designed to probe the interviewees' experiences beyond that congregation. Frankly, I did not expect to gain much insight from these questions.

Much to my surprise, a question concerning congregations in which the members of that congregation had been active formerly elicited a definite pattern of responses. The majority of the members had transferred from small, city or rural congregations, mostly of the same denomination. The insight struck me when I saw the data, "This church is growing more as a result of where it is located than as a consequence of what its leaders are doing." Then the related thought followed: "Those city and country churches are losing members more because of where they are located than because of what their leaders are doing."

For the first time I saw a pattern, bigger than I—than all of us. During the past several decades there has been a massive circulation of members out of small, city and rural churches into suburban churches for reasons that had little to do with what the particular congregations did or did not do. Some congregations have gained and others have suffered from the effects of what sociologists call "geographical and social mobility." The church may not be of the world, but neither can it escape the world.

An appreciation of the effects of social change is needed if one is to develop realistic expectations for small churches. The evidence is all around us, both in city neighborhoods and in rural areas. During the years I served as a small-church pastor and, later, as synod executive I watched the change take place. Agriculture became mechanized and centralized, and in the process the number of farm families was drastically reduced. Local creameries and family farms merged or went out of business. Our family farm in Maine is an example; although today it cannot fully support us, at one time it did support a leading community family in considerable affluence for many years.

With the drop in population, crossroad stores gave way to stores in villages; ultimately, these yielded to chain supermarkets in shopping centers located on the outskirts of large villages. In much the same manner, crossroad churches gave way to churches in the villages; only the strongest of these survive today.

Like it or not, people have had to go with change to survive. For many, forced relocation is an unwelcome consequence. With a shrinking economic base, many communities cannot support as many persons as in the past.

The drop in population has affected the mainline denominations and their congregations the most. The families that comprise these congregations usually have the means and the desire to give their children the benefits of education. More and more, children from these families leave the community to pursue higher education and then, when they return, discover they are educated beyond the community's capacity to provide them with challenging work. The withdrawal of these young persons from the nonmetropolitan areas has meant a steady loss of young adults from the old churches. Many small mainline congregations in rural areas are now composed mostly of middle-aged and older persons.

Not everyone has the capacity or the desire to relocate. Those without the means or with less incentive to seek higher education are most likely to remain in rural communities. The lot of rural congregations who serve those who choose not to relocate has—not too surprisingly—often improved. Many are not aware of this improvement, because it does not normally appear in the statistics of mainline denominations. Most mainline congregations represent a social status, a theology, and a way of life that are not amenable to the majority of those who stay in rural areas. In fact, many of these persons affirm a way of life that runs counter to the overall trend of mainstream culture and enter this culture only when necessary.

That persons of such a viewpoint seek a congregation that stands independent of the mainstream culture is not surprising. A church that is over against the larger world fits their life-style, because its theology and polity tend to be uncomplex, straightforward, and individual-oriented.

Conservative and independent congregations prosper in such a social context. Currently, for example, on a typical

Sunday morning in Maine more people worship in independent, nonaligned congregations than in *all* congregations attached to all denominations combined.

Edward Hassinger and John Holik identify a similar pattern, favoring more conservative, sect-type congregations over mainline denominational congregations, in their study of rural Missouri. During a fifteen-year period church-type congregations in rural areas of that state show a 7.4 percent loss; in the same time span independent, sect-type congregations show a 4.2 percent gain.[1] Regardless of the region of the United States in which they are located, rural congregations from mainline denominations have seen their membership erode as scores of young people who, in a former time, would have stayed in the community now move up economically and away geographically. All this social change has happened despite an increase in the number of effective leaders and programs in many of these congregations.

Losses in the City

A pattern much like that observed in rural areas appears in many city neighborhoods as well. The causes are strikingly similar. I experienced the effects of urban social change directly when I lived in the inner city of Albany, New York. Originally, my home neighborhood was St. Anthony's parish. I lived up the street from St. Anthony's church and school buildings. Now both are vacant, victims of the migration of Italians from the neighborhood. The majority of the small number of Italians who remain—like a neighbor, Mr. Ali—are old. Of the persons who live there now, the greatest proportion are blacks; the neighborhood also contains a generous sprinkling of Spanish-speaking persons and a few newly arrived whites, many of whom are renovating the two- and three-storied brownstones.

With the exception of one or two stalwart survivors, the

mainline Protestant churches there have all suffered the same fate as St. Anthony's. They were all founded long before the Italian immigration that St. Anthony's was built to serve. Most of the Protestant congregations had dwindled to a remnant and finally closed their doors long before the 1950s. Most of their members redistributed themselves into suburban churches or dropped out. I traced the pattern of redistribution systematically in my chapter in *Understanding Church Growth and Decline: 1950-1978*.[2]

A key chart from that study, which appears on page 10, groups United Methodist, United Presbyterian, and Reformed Church in America congregations according to their relative distances from the inner city. Inner Urban Neighborhood congregations (Type 3) are closest to the center city, whereas Metropolitan Suburb congregations (Type 6) are farthest from the inner city. Beginning as early as the turn of the century, decline follows growth in mainline congregations as one moves through the years and away from the city centers toward the outer suburbs. By the end of the period charted (1975) Type 3 congregations had lost 5,500 members, whereas Type 6 congregations had gained 4,500 members. As noted, those "lost" and those "gained" were, in many cases, the same persons; they simply transferred. While only a few urban centers are combined in the chart, I have seen the same general pattern within many urban centers across North America.

Of course, not everyone moves out; like the rural areas, some stay and others move in. The fate of a congregation depends on how well it meets the needs of those who are available or how well it adapts to do so. Often parked one or two spaces away from my car on the street would be a large, green car with a "Pastor" bumper sticker. I cannot recall the exact name of the congregation this pastor serves, but I remember that it contains the word apostolic and that it is not affiliated with a denomination. It is a small, urban ver-

Combined Church Membership by Type
(United Presbyterian, United Methodist, and Reformed Church in America)

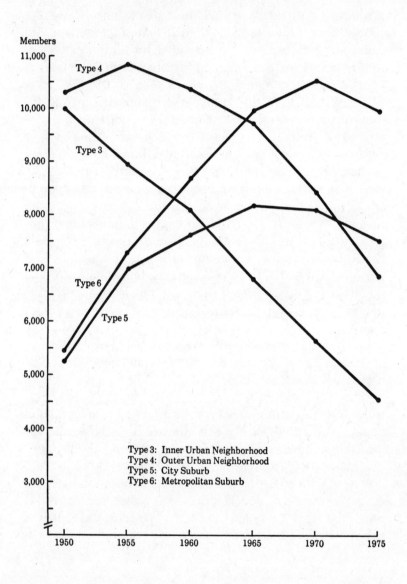

Members

Type 4

Type 3

Type 6

Type 5

Type 3: Inner Urban Neighborhood
Type 4: Outer Urban Neighborhood
Type 5: City Suburb
Type 6: Metropolitan Suburb

sion of the independent congregations that are multiplying in rural areas.

I have studied a host of these new, smaller congregations over the past few years and have found that while many of them would like to be larger, they do not experience being small as a problem in the same ways as mainline congregations do. Pastors of these independent congregations in the city typically derive part of their support from non-church-related employment. Such congregations often meet in modest buildings and therefore do not carry the oppressive overhead many dwindled mainline congregations do.

Those of us who are aligned with mainline congregations have customarily termed these congregations marginal. We are discovering that the definition of marginal depends on where one thinks the center is supposed to be. In fact, I argue below that our thriving as mainline congregations will involve emulating some of the survival tactics used by those whom many of us view as untypical and marginal.

To summarize: Social change almost entirely beyond the control of congregations and their leaders has had immense impact on both rural and urban small churches. I think this impact is habitually underestimated. Our biases encourage us to blame our program or ourselves, more than the changed environment within which we must live, for the adversities our congregations suffer. The tendency to blame someone for not trying hard enough or for following the wrong strategy only compounds the problem. It steers us away from the real task to which we need to give attention: understanding and learning to cope within the social environment that is really there.

Misguided Strategies

Inaccurate perceptions lead to misguided strategies. For strategies to be helpful to a congregation they must fit the social context within which the members of that congregation live. Unfortunately, many of the strategies recently developed to help small churches were drawn from the very culture that the members of those small churches were seeking to avoid.

Somewhere along the way many church leaders apparently decided that small congregations, in order to survive, would have to conform to the overall direction mainstream society was taking. Those who wanted a small congregation would need to be educated to the realities of a time that rendered small congregations organizationally unworkable. They would need to catch up. By this logic, being small became the big problem to overcome. The line of thinking then developed in the following manner.

If being small was the problem, obviously we leaders needed to help small congregations become bigger. Usually, the language was more technical; we talked of the need to "enlarge the congregation's base of support." So we amalgamated in a growing variety of ways, from yokes to clusters to larger parishes to mergers. Often we proceeded regretfully, but we sighed and went ahead in the belief that the times were rendering small congregations economically and programmatically untenable. Church members would have to adjust. The fact that much of the time they did not embrace our strategies willingly did not deter us. Two simple truths escaped us: (1) Most of the people who participate in small congregations do so because the congregation is small, and (2) when a congregation becomes large it is less able to meet these people's needs.

We chose to explain our limited success with a second methodological assumption based in mainstream culture: We needed to improve our technique. To solve the small-church problem, we sought to plan better, manage better, administrate better, deal better with conflict or stewardship or evangelism, each time hoping a better-applied technique would arrest the losses and lead the small church closer toward becoming a more viable, larger (and compliant) church.

To implement the needed strategies, clergy would have to adopt a new perspective and see themselves primarily as professionals. In line with a culture losing confidence in piety, clergy were encouraged to become competent practitioners. As achievement became the society's cardinal value, ministers were increasingly judged on their ability to *do,* to accomplish. The congregation was viewed as the group with which the minister was to do something. The group's worth (theological word: faithfulness) was judged on some standard the minister had learned elsewhere and that he or she then brought to the group and up to which the group was supposed to measure. The congregation that resisted cooperation, that would not grow or change as it was "supposed to" was commonly viewed as a "problem" by pastor and denomination. The bind was very real. The pastor, to be successful, had to make the congregation change. In most cases, success would ultimately be found elsewhere, because as we have seen, social conditions—not leadership and/or program—had the greatest influence on whether any church could grow in these years.

The fourth development was an unsought consequence: Fascination with the methods of behavioral science drew our attention away from seeking that spiritual enrichment without which no congregation can be a church and no clergyperson a minister. The most striking change in small mainline congregations in this century is their loss of a spirituality that addresses the lives of their members. As a friend observed to me in the midst of the era, "The real problem in the church today is that no one knows for sure what it means

[13]

to be spiritual anymore." The social context for which we had a congruent spirituality has changed substantially. All our behavioral-science-based wisdom has not compensated for our lack of spiritual integrity. We have hardly begun to address this problem, and more than likely it is the core problem in the church today.

Looking back, then, we can see that much of our frustration in the small congregation can be traced to two interrelated factors:

First, we underestimated both the effects of social change as causes of the difficulties that beset small churches and the power of church leaders to cope with these effects.

Second, we drew the methods designed to help small congregations from the mainstream culture alien to most small-church members.

We need to heed these lessons learned from the past as we move ahead. To ignore or seek to escape from the realities of social change is foolish. We do not have the power to escape social change. At the same time, strategies we advocate to help congregations cope must be congruent with the subculture within which their members live. What church members of a particular congregation want—that is, what they will support—is as much a given as the economic resources available to them. Many are willing to adjust their wants *as necessary,* but most of the time they need to see the adjustments as necessary in order to go along with them. When we force on a congregation strategies that are substantially out of line with what the members want, many of these members will either go elsewhere to find what they want or drop out of church altogether. Such is the difference between power and authority. Authority is based on consent.

Moving Ahead

I suggest we seek appropriate strategies for our work in small congregations by drawing, first of all, on the insights of

[14]

two representative persons who have always been members of small congregations. I choose to begin here because I believe that the methods we employ with any congregation, in order to be safe and effective, need to fit within the culture of that congregation. The two representatives show us how the values of the congregation need to be considered and how we can go about developing strategies that are in harmony with the life-style of a small congregation.

I met the first of these two persons some years ago, while working with small congregations as a synod executive. He rang my telephone frequently during the sixties and early seventies, seeking to enlist my energies to resist two trends he saw as undermining the well-being of small churches.

One of the trends this person opposed was that more and more our denomination took the position of helping clergy at the expense of congregations, especially in the matter of increasing and mandated salary minimums. It puzzled him that our policy seemed to value clergy more than congregations, because we regularly raised the amount churches had to pay to have full-time ministers without offering what he considered effective help to increase the churches' ability to support full-time ministers. All the helps we offered insisted that the churches move toward some kind of organizational amalgamation—which he regarded the least desirable solution. Why were we so unwilling to consider alternative styles for ministers while insisting that churches make prescribed organizational adjustments simply to support increasingly expensive pastors? I thought he had been seeing matters one-sidedly and told him so. But none of my explanations could counter his view that we valued clergy more than congregations. If the congregations were suffering hard times, why should the clergy be immune to this suffering, he wanted to know. Our organizational efforts to guarantee the clergy's immunity did not seem to him to be Christian.

The other trend to which my friend objected he saw as being related, namely, the effort of ministers to gain acceptance as professionals. To him, this appeared to place ministers on a level with doctors and lawyers, which he viewed (in a noneconomic context) as a step *down*. He saw ministers as "men of God" (no women were ordained in my denomination in those days) and considered them valuable because of what they *are*, not—like other professionals—because of what they can *do*. To him, the difference was pivotal, even if subtle. He said it most clearly one day in an outburst: "If a minister can't inspire, I don't care what else he can do!"

That remark threw me headlong down a historical flight of stairs. What did those memorable pastors do throughout all the centuries that is so memorable? They inspired! Perhaps the core issue of clergy identity today is not occupational, but spiritual? We shall look straight at this question presently.

In those former days it was not likely my friend would have seen himself as a harbinger of the times ahead. But he was—economically, socially, and spiritually.

Year by year we are steadily losing economic capacity. Everywhere, including in the church, fewer resources are available to us. Most of us, including clergy, cannot look forward to lives of increasing abundance. I doubt that the church can maintain its spiritual integrity before the world if it adopts a policy of protecting clergy against the economic reverses nearly everyone else is suffering.

Many who belong to the generation now moving into middle adulthood hold new attitudes and values. The increasing incidence of their movement away from the suburb to rural areas or city neighborhoods illustrates the difference. Both economics and values motivate the shift. Many seek less complex lives as well as neighborhoods that contain a mixture of economic levels and, sometimes, ethnic groups. Most persons who are in their thirties today are more realistic than the previous generation about the limited economic opportunities of the emerging era.

The directness of the new generation can challenge congregation and pastor alike. An increasing body of research indicates that adults in this age-group respect clergy most who can inspire (perhaps because the major need of the time is hope?). Also, when such persons do seek a church, many—if not most—seek a congregation that will address their spiritual needs.[3]

That search poses a crisis. Little has been done to improve or update the spiritual capacity of most small congregations. Loren Mead defines the dilemma clearly in his commentary on the Washington County Mission Program, a fine effort by the Episcopal Church to help small parishes. He wonders:

> As I read about the people of these three congregations I see solid signs of increased commitment and involvement in the life of the congregation and I also think I see signs of some people doing some growing as individuals in their relationship to God. Are these things related? Is the focus on organizational effectiveness likely to be seductive as it often becomes in larger congregations, sometimes even becoming a substitute for religious effectiveness? Forgive me for that phrase, "religious effectiveness," but I don't know how to say it otherwise. Is the work to get people "involved" related to helping people to face into their own nature under God, searching out their own vocations, and working out their own salvation?[4]

That religious or, as I prefer to call it, "spiritual effectiveness" is precisely what is basic to the church, *and* the times call for now. Yet we rarely address it. Most of the time we analyze, reorganize, plan, and reprogram. In the process we seldom ask the basic questions related to spiritual effectiveness. How can this congregation help people live as Christians? What is getting in its way of doing that? What kind of leader do we need to help us witness to our faith where we live every day? These *are* pivotal issues. If a minister cannot inspire, does it matter what else he or she

[17]

can do? And if a minister *can* inspire, everything else she or he can do matters more.

An Artful Helper

How can we help a small congregation discover and develop its unique strengths? That question leads to my second source of insight. As the crusty elder confronts us with the necessity to keep the basic needs of a congregation as a church foremost, the second person illustrates how we can inspire a small church to overcome its problems by developing its strengths.

That person is Mr. Churchill—not Sir Winston; I do not think he ever told me his first name. I met him because of a sick tree, which had leafed out poorly at the top for a few years. I talked about the tree with a friend who was more familiar with the locale than I, inquiring about someone who might be able to help. He said he knew of only two persons who did that kind of work: one was a botanist who was associated with the science department at a nearby university and the other was Mr. Churchill, who lived in a small village in the opposite direction. So far as my friend knew, the botanist was competent—and expensive. Mr. Churchill was not as expensive but was a character. Even so, many people preferred him.

In the midst of earning a graduate degree at the time, I called the botanist, and he arrived late in the afternoon for a "consultation," on his way home from the university. He gazed solemnly at the tree. Yes, it was diseased, obviously the result of an infestation of insects that carried the disease into the top of the tree, where the leaves were stunted and falling off. There was hope, however; the tree could be saved. He knew of one chemical that would kill the bugs and of another that would arrest the progress of the disease, but it would take several treatments. The cost would be about

[18]

one hundred dollars per treatment, or about four hundred dollars in all, depending on how the tree responded. He could guarantee nothing and said he should start the treatments without delay.

He was annoyed when I told him I wanted to obtain a second opinion and most especially when I mentioned this opinion was to be offered by Mr. Churchill. But I persisted.

Churchill arrived at 8:30 the next morning. He appeared to be in his late fifties, weather-beaten, but still strong. "Churchill's my name," he said, as he gripped my hand. "This the tree?" I nodded. "Well, let's have a look." He stood there for a time and pondered the tree. Then he looked at me with searching eyes and asked a question for which I was totally unprepared: "Do you love your tree?"

"Why . . . of course!" I stammered, the overstatement obviously an attempt to compensate for my hesitancy.

"Then I'll see what I can do." He walked back to his truck and returned with a pair of binoculars. He looked at the tree from various angles. "Just as I suspected," he said. "You can't tell much about a tree from a distance." Again he walked back to his truck and this time returned with a set of climbing spurs attached to his heavy boots. He proceeded to climb the massive tree, all the way up into the thin-leafed top, higher than the roof on my Victorian house. I scrambled about to avoid the pieces of dead wood that tumbled down as he climbed upward.

Soon he was back on the ground. "Well, the tree's got problems," he said. "When did the lightning strike it?" I replied that I had not known lightning struck it. "Well, it did," he went on, "and a damn good thing the tree was there, because if it hadn't been, that lightning would have hit your house and probably burned it to the ground. Your tree's done you more good than you realize.

"Anyway, the tree's had a big wound ever since then and the life's been running out of it. The leaves are stunted because the good strength they need is running out of the wound. I can dress the wound, and then when the tree heals, the good strength will get back to the upper branches. Of course, we'll need to take out a few branches. A weakened tree can't support all that overgrowth; it doesn't really need it anyway."

"What about the bugs?" I asked, pointing to several crawling out of the dead wood. "Don't you have to get rid of the bugs?"

"That scientist from the university's been here hasn't he?" I confessed that he had. "Well, he's a smart fellow, I suppose; we just don't agree on much. Them scientists work mostly with bugs in bottles. Hell, killing bugs in bottles is no trick. The trick is to kill the bugs without hurting the tree and to kill the bad bugs and not the good bugs. I'll sweep the bugs out of the wound and then dress it, to keep them out. When the tree gets stronger the bugs won't bother it anymore. And you won't have all the sick birds around that you'd have if somebody started feeding the bugs chemicals. Once you start spreading those chemicals around you lose control of where they'll go."

I was becoming convinced. "Do you need to do anything more with the tree?" I asked.

"Like I said, dress the wound and prune away the dead branches. Then we need to feed it some fertilizer. You can't expect a tree to heal itself if you don't feed it."

"When can you do the work and how much will it cost me?" I asked.

He could tell I was a bit nervous. He looked at the old house and then back at me. "You make much money?" he inquired.

"No," I replied. "I'm a minister."

"Then it'll cost you ninety dollars. Can you afford ninety dollars?"

"Yes."

"You got ninety dollars right now?"

"Yes, I do."

"Well, then I can do the work right now." Which he did.

Mr. Churchill had a boy with him who was about fourteen years old and whom he introduced simply as Charlie. For the next two hours he and Charlie kept a feverish pace, he in the tree and Charlie dodging the falling branches (and once the chain saw Mr. Churchill accidentally dropped from the top of the tree) and attaching tools and supplies to ropes to be hauled up into the tree. Finally, Churchill walked around the tree, drilling holes a foot deep with a heavy bar. Charlie followed close behind, filling each hole with fertilizer. They finished before lunchtime and I paid Mr. Churchill ninety dollars. I never saw him again. The tree recovered quite nicely just like he said it would. The bugs, by the way, gave up.

Home-grown Strategies

Mr. Churchill provides surprisingly appropriate guidance for those of us concerned about understanding how to work effectively with small congregations. I confess that I reviewed my life as a pastor and synod executive during the three hours I spent with him. How I wish I had met him ten years earlier! I continue year by year to be refreshed by his wisdom. Let me share some suggestions he stimulates.

The attitude we take when we define a church's problem influences the primary solution we propose. Is our major objective to kill the bugs or is it to strengthen the tree? Each objective leads toward a different outcome.

A strategy designed to kill the bugs can easily result in overkill (kill off the good bugs along with the bad). I have seen the results of that kind of strategy all too often in my work as a consultant. One example can serve as typical. I was called in to discover why two congregations that had merged had, in three years, resulted in a new congregation with fewer members than the smaller of the two original churches. I found that the merger had been forced, to wrest control from a few dissident members (the bad bugs). But about sixty healthy members had also refused to go along with the merger. Most told stories of being overlooked, their needs discounted by those in charge. Some now attend other churches; many do not attend church at all. The dissidents are gone, but so is the equivalent of one church. The strategy worked but, in my opinion, did more harm than good.

When people support a church year after year they probably do so because it contributes something valuable to their lives. We need to be in touch with what that contribution is *before* we can safely suggest changes, especially if it is a congregation with whom we do not live week by week.

Often a congregation has hidden assets and strengths apparent only at close range. "The tree's done you more good than you realize." The outside consultant or denominational representative who comes to work with a small congregation is, initially, more familiar with the strategies he or she has to offer than with how the hidden strengths of that particular congregation are being wasted. "The tree's had a big wound ever since then and the life's been running out of it." Sometimes the outsider's bias leads him or her to force a congregation to adopt alien procedures rather than find and bind up its wounds and then help it draw on its inherent strength.

Alien procedures are usually difficult for local leaders to use. One of the more frustrating experiences I remember from my years as a synod executive was the inability of most congregations to utilize the programs and resources I developed. After a while I even stopped thinking the fact they could not use them was their fault! Then I listened. One pastor described the difficulty lucidly: "We are really worse off after the training sessions, because now we know how we should do it and we still can't make it work." A major theme of Dr. Willard Gaylin's recent book, *Feelings*,[5] argues that we human beings are more complex and individual than the popular psychological therapies now in vogue would lead us to believe. So are small congregations. The leaders of the small churches in my synod were not saying my abilities to classify and program were no good. They were pointing out that most of the time strategies built on standardized models are alien to a congregation. Such strategies do not go deep enough to probe a church's individuality, and because they are unnatural to a congregation, they usually do not abide. Someone who stays long enough and gets close enough to bind wounds and nurture a congregation's inherent strength is more helpful.

The inherent strength of a congregation is what it is willing to give itself to. That may not be what the outsider thinks the members ought to attend to first, but then their greater familiarity with their church usually makes their judgment superior. I recall, for example, working with one small congregation that, from my point of view, needed most of all to grow. Accordingly, I suggested some church-growth strategies. The people were cold to my ideas. They wanted to build up their ability to nurture family life. That seemed, to me, to be a step in the wrong direction (in not out). But I went along with their wishes and found someone to help them do what *they* thought they should do first. In the end their enhanced ability to nurture family life attracted a host of new members. Following their judgment freed up an abiding capacity to sustain growth.

It is easier to view a congregation as dispensable when one is not a member of that congregation. The clinical viewpoint that comes more naturally to the outsider is *not* more desirable than the personal viewpoint held by the insider. A healthy tension exists between the two viewpoints. In fact, each of us needs that tension within us when we work with a small congregation.

We can reword Mr. Churchill's opening question and then profitably address ourselves with it: "Do you love this congregation?" If we cannot answer "Yes" for a congregation, I doubt whether we should attempt to work with that congregation. When we become too clinical or dispassionate in our attitude toward a congregation, we cannot make sound decisions relating to that congregation.

The danger in giving too much power to those with a purely clinical attitude is the detachment that attitude encourages. If we cannot feel with a congregation, we cannot work responsibly with that congregation. In my experience, often a congregation will sense the lack of feeling and take steps to protect itself—and rightly so. My elder friend sensed a dispassionate using of congregations by denominations and was seeking to protect his congregation from that abuse.

Please do not misunderstand me at this point. I am *not* advocating that *every* church should be kept alive at *all* costs. Churches, like people, can reach a point where even though they maintain a few body functions they are really dead. It makes no sense to spend massive resources for heroic measures to sustain a church in such a state. In these moments the differing perspectives of outside helper and local member are equally vital. Otherwise, closing a church can be a nasty and brutal business. It does not have to be. On occasion I have been the outsider present with those who have seen their church pass into a state where only heroic measures could keep it alive. I have been present when the only course seemed to be to give up a beloved building where children's children had been baptized. Usually these people weep. Sometimes I do too. And my elder friend's words have come back to me: "If a minister can't inspire, I don't care what else he [or she] can do." Competence should not be discounted. At the same time, it cannot substitute for faith or love.

It is usually best to work within the resources available locally to a congregation and pastor. Mr. Churchill framed what he chose to do within the resources he thought I had. Then he asked me, "Can you afford ninety dollars?" and went ahead after I told him I could.

The time of looking forward to endless support or even to significant economic support from outside for small congregations is over. A more realistic attitude is "What can we do with what we have?"

The two major sources of economic enslavement for small congregations is the pastor's support and building maintenance. Typically, the denomination is most resistant to cutbacks in the former; the local church, to cutbacks in the latter. With the end of affluence setting severe limits on the economic capability of most denominations, we need to make do with what we have both for ministers and for church buildings.

The trend is apparent. Upward of one quarter of all clergy now earn a portion of their support beyond their congregations. Others serve a small congregation by voluntarily making significant economic sacrifice. I admire them. Some years ago I told a congregation seeking a new pastor, "You will get what you are willing to pay for." What a terrible capitulation to affluent, secular values! Certainly no denomination can be said to be exercising its responsibility when it permits the members of a congregation to set their contribution to a minister's salary lower than they obviously can afford. To imply that clergy are substandard who earn a portion of their support elsewhere in order to serve a small church or who choose to live on what a church can afford seems equally abusive.

The central criteria for a clergyperson is how obviously that person's life witnesses to the Christian faith and how effectively that person ministers to others in the role of an ordained minister. Whether the minister does so within a congregation of ten or a thousand or is fully or only partly supported by the church is not nearly as significant as whether his or her life and ministry challenge and support others to grow as Christians. I have met some full- and part-time ministers who were effective and others of both types who were not. The nature of their economic support was by no means the critical distinguishing factor. In the emerging age, with its economic limits, more ministers will have to make do because more congregations will have to make do.

We can see the trend in changing patterns of building utilization, especially by smaller congregations. With the rising costs of heating and cooling, many congregations have become more honest and innovative about space use. In many instances the by-products have been surprisingly beneficial. Some congregations have discovered a new closeness of fellowship by gathering throughout the winter in easier-to-heat church basements or in homes for Sunday school and for other church meetings. Others have found a new richness by joining with other congregations for worship in the hard-to-heat (or cool) season. In the coming years more and more congregations will seek to form cooperative relationships for their survival and will look for experienced and sensitive outside resource persons to help them do so.

Such is the nature of the social context in which we will live, which brings us back to where we began—facing the immense power of social change. We have looked at some misguided efforts to help small congregations cope and have attempted to learn from these mistakes. Moving on, we have sought guidance from persons who represent the subculture of smaller congregations. Finally, we have defined some appropriate strategies for use with small congregations in the present and emerging future.

Along the way I hope we have appreciated the great resilience of the small church. Given the trends of our time that honor the hardiness of those who can do well with what they have, I expect we will all gain much from the many vital and suprisingly relevant small congregations.

2

Worship in the Small Congregation

Paul Gibson

From the point of view of worship, the small congregation is normative.

The roots of Christian worship are in the synagogue and in the ritual meals of Judaism; the former required ten worshipers and the latter, only a family or an informal group of comparable size.

The temple, with its great size, vast space, ranks of clergy, and massed choirs, was not the model for Christian worship. It was a model for much symbolism and theology, but not for the worship of the early church.

It is true that Jesus frequented the temple, but only as a place to proclaim his gospel. His ambivalent attitude toward the temple was cited at his trial.

Jesus was not ambivalent about the synagogue. Luke tells the story of Jesus' attendance at the sabbath service in Nazareth (4:16-30). He makes a point of letting his readers know that Jesus went regularly to the synagogue on the sabbath day. That particular service nearly ended in a lynching. But in the very next passage we see Jesus back in a synagogue, this time in Capernaum (4:31-32).

Jesus was not ambivalent about the ritual meals. The importance of the worship meals celebrated with his disciples shines out in the long discourse that John has left to us. Luke's account of the Last Supper (22:14-15) preserves the intensity of value placed on those experiences: "When the hour came, he sat at table, and the apostles with him. And he said to them, 'I have earnestly desired to eat this passover with you before I suffer.'"

At the breaking of bread in the village called Emmaus only three people were present (Luke 24:13-44). And yet that story, with its opening of the scriptures and its recognition of the risen Lord in the eucharistic bread, is perhaps the primary model of Christian worship in the whole of the New Testament.

The only really large liturgical event one encounters in the New Testament is the baptism of three thousand, on the day of Pentecost (Acts 2:41). But that occasion was unique and charismatic and not normative. Early Christians continued to go to the temple for daily prayers (Acts 2:46), and we are told it was Paul's custom to go to the synagogue on the sabbath (Acts 17:2), but specifically, Christian worship rotated around the breaking of bread in private houses.

The *dimensions* of early Christian worship were defined by its context, which was domestic. The *shape* of the worshiping community, including its emerging leadership functions, was probably inspired by the synagogue. Both influences suggest a known community, highly participatory in its activity, rather than a large, impersonal assembly.

We may trace the growth of the Christian community through the remains of its architecture. Early Christian worship took place in ordinary houses. When Christians first wanted separate and distinct places for assembly and worship, they either adapted private houses or erected buildings modeled on private houses. Dom Gregory Dix has demonstrated the suitability of the Roman patrician house for

Christian assembly. It was essentially an embellishment of the ancient Roman farmstead. All the old elements were there: The old log cabin had become an inner room, the old chopping block had become a fixed stone table, and the original well had become an ornamental pool, still to be found in an open space (now pillared but still skylit) between the entrance and the inner room where, in pagan homes, the gods of the hearth were to be found. All this could be "christianized" with little difficulty: The pool became font and the table became altar; the father's chair became the bishop's throne; the community of worshipers stood around, giving tangible expression to the prayer in the old Latin canon of the mass for *omnium circumstantium*.[1]

At Dura-Europos, in Syria, a noteworthy house-church has been discovered, where in A.D. 232, a wall was removed between two rooms to make space for the eucharistic assembly and a third room was turned into a baptistery.[2] Another house-church—the "titulus Equitii"—is in Rome. It is only "a house containing a room used as a place of reunion by the faithful."[3]

All this assumed a small congregation, a community capable of intimacy and mutual support, whose worship belonged to its members and was their responsibility.

The movement to large congregations was the result of the conversion of large numbers of people. The legalization of Christianity, in the fourth century, accelerated the process. Small congregations were not possible or could be maintained only with great difficulty. Larger buildings symbolized the change and froze the movement's efforts.

When Christians needed larger buildings they turned away from the domestic house as a model and adopted the basilica, the building used for the local assembly hall and the courthouse in ancient Rome. The basilica was rectangular, divided by pillars into three aisles, with a semicircular apse at the end. It made possible larger congregations as well as more disconnected congregations. When the imperial basilica was used as a courthouse the magistrate sat in a chair in the apse and the lawyers gathered in a restricted area near him; his place was now taken by the bishop (especially in the Roman and North African adaptations of the basilica), and the clergy surrounded him. Later, in the fourth century, when monks began to appear in considerable numbers in the urban churches, they occupied the place between the altar and the people. As a worshiping community, the church had been multidimensional; now the various functions of the different members were becoming isolating.

Many movements of the Reformation attempted to address the problem of fragmented and disengaged worship and, in some cases, were able to unite their efforts to a folk tradition that recovered a sense of belonging, of ownership, of participation even in very small congregations. Where these movements have prevailed, and especially where they have been open to the perennial need for a liturgy that embraces and expresses itself in terms of the current culture, we can only give thanks. But the worship of many small congregations seems second-best even to the participants. And because of the baggage of history and the lack of self-confidence it generates, such worship may be second-best. Country people have often felt dismissed by city people; the small is easily intimidated, not least in its own estimation of self-worth. But in the area of Christian worship the small congregation has no need to apologize: The small congregation is where it all began, and everything that is authentic to Christian liturgy is available to it.

Some Principles

Robert Hovda has argued that the three irreducible elements of the Sunday observance of early Christians are the gathering, the sense of being called and equipped for a common mission, and the breaking of bread. The congregation must be small enough for these elements to have a sense of reality, for them to be experienced existentially and not just representationally.[4] (This is not to attack the symbolic, but to distinguish between living symbols and "mere" symbols, which actually inoculate against contact with that which they claim to represent.)

At this point we need to identify some principles of liturgy and worship that may be tested against the reality of the small congregation and, if appropriate, used to reform and strengthen its life.

First, we need to examine the words we are using. The words liturgy and worship have carried many meanings in their long histories (the first comes from Greek and the second from Anglo-Saxon). It may be necessary to be a little arbitrary in tying them down to specific meanings for a precise conversation.

"Liturgy" carries from its origins the sense of "the work of the people" or "a public work." At one time it was used to refer to the generous action of a citizen on behalf of the community, e.g., the building of a road or the erection of a shrine. Christians have, from an early date, used the word liturgy to stand for those actions of proclamation, prayer, and thanksgiving for which they regularly gather.

"Worship" is an action or attitude that affirms the great worth of its object. Mayors and magistrates may, in some jurisdictions, be called "your Worship," not to treat them as gods, but because of the dignity inherent in the office they hold in the community. Worship offered to God affirms the infinite love and mercy of the Creator and Redeemer. Worship is God's glory reflected by a thankful creation. Because "the glory of God is humanity fully alive," the worship of God is secured ultimately not in subjective experiences of piety (important as these may be as part of the picture), but

[32]

in whole men and women joined in a just society, using their world with thanksgiving and responsibility.

Worship therefore includes liturgy, but liturgy does not include worship. Worship is the whole of life insofar as it reflects the glory of God; liturgy is the sign that points the way to worship, the lens that concentrates its burning heat, the small symbol that makes the larger landscape visible, the map that makes it possible to be committed to the journey.

A second principle is that God does not need liturgy. This principle, central to the biblical themes that were ultimately and uniquely expressed in the person, message, and work of Jesus Christ, is frequently forgotten by the church (although historically, it may have been the fuel of much reformation).

Amos, in 5:21-24, makes the point very clear:

> I hate, I despise your feasts,
>   and I take no delight in your solemn assemblies.
> Even though you offer me your burnt offerings
>   and cereal offerings,
>   I will not accept them,
> and the peace offerings of your fatted beasts
>   I will not look upon.
> Take away from me the noise of your songs;
>   to the melody of your harps I will not listen.
> But let justice roll down like waters,
>   and righteousness like an everlasting stream.

Clearly, what God requires is not liturgy, but worship in the fullest sense of the word: righteousness, love, mercy, justice, the fully alive response of men and women who yearn for the coming of God's reign.

When Jesus' disciples asked why he ate with people who were ritually unclean, he added even more force to this line of thought. He answered (Matthew 9:12): "Those who are well have no need of a physician, but those who are sick. Go and learn what this means, 'I desire mercy, and not sacrifice.'"

In light of this prophetic judgment we must assert that, taken in itself, liturgy has no value whatsoever. God does not need it. It is not inherently important. To invest the rites, myths, enclosures, and roles of liturgy with a sacral worth of their own is to absolutize the relative, and this is idolatry. Thus far even an Anglican can embrace the Protestant abhorrence of ceremonialism.

Taken in terms of its function, however, liturgy is of inestimable value. It is like the map that is not itself the pilgrimage, but without which the quest will be in vain. It is like rear-vision mirrors which enable us to orient ourselves in traffic and which save us from the restricted and dangerous impression that there is nothing on the journey but ourselves and the road ahead. It is like poetry that looks obliquely into the texture of experience, not just analytically.

Liturgy is constantly found between the poles of greatest value and worthlessness. It is neither a compromise of those terms nor their product. It is always both. If we take up residence in liturgy, we become detached, disconnected, angelistic, immoral (because ethics are rooted in blood-and-dust experience), and, eventually, silly. But if we ignore liturgy, we risk losing the very capacity for sensitivity to that blood-and-dust experience, we risk losing our human roots. The ritualist is like someone with new glasses who is so preoccupied with the lenses and their effect that she does not see what they are intended to make clear. The iconoclast denies that he needs glasses at all.

God does not need liturgy; people do need liturgy in order to discover what God does require to enter into it.

At this point we may note that the distinction between liturgical and nonliturgical churches is false. Liturgy is what churches do to discover and rediscover the Christian "way." Different traditions have developed liturgy in different ways—with different degrees of rigidity, with different attitudes to the aesthetic as a modality of the sacred—but in every tradition there are recurring patterns and themes. Even the most "free" tradition is still a tradition (it was handed down), and there is a finite limit to the range of the unexpected. Even silence is a negative form, capturing as in a mold those terms and reflections of commitment that in another tradition would be more positively articulated.

Can we identify the elements of liturgy that are common to our various traditions? Yes, we can, and they are common not only to Christian denominations, but to the universal manifestation of what we call religion. They are rite and myth, action and story, something done and something said. Rite and myth are the building blocks of religion, the stuff of which its foundations are made. Rite grows out of those primitive (yet still present) actions that people perform at times of jarring change, times that we have identified by the word passage, times when the experience of life and death and transition lays bare the radical ambiguity of the human experience. Myth is the means by which a people preserve and tell their story, locating themselves in an otherwise confused and tangled continuum in time, finding their roots behind the earliest recorded historical event and their hopes beyond the foreseeable future.

Rite and myth (i.e., liturgy) are the means by which people seek a place of congruence with an ambiguously experienced universe. They will not find the answer to their search in liturgy; they will find it only in life. But they may find the key in liturgy.

We must avoid a simplistic identification of rite (thing done) with sacrament and of myth (story told) with word. The Christian liturgies of word and sacrament are complete liturgies; each is composed of both rite and myth. The liturgical celebration of the word is something done as well as something said; the proclamation of the story is itself an action, a rite, and its ritual nature is enhanced by the setting of hymns and songs, interpretation, and formal prayer of deep concern in which it is experienced in virtually every Christian tradition. Similarly, sacramental liturgies are not bare actions, tantric gestures devoid of intelligible content; they are vital precisely because they are done in conjunction with the telling of the story for the anamnesis (literally, the "not having amnesia about") of the saving person and event.

The complementarity of word and sacrament is secured by the fully liturgical nature of each; each emphasizes one of the poles of liturgy and at the same time includes the essential nature of the other.

The origin of liturgy in the twilight dawn of the emergence of our species guarantees the essential humanity of the exercise. (I hypothesize that the funeral procession is the primal religious act: the carrying of the body out of the camp in despair and the return to the camp in grief and hope.) For the Christian, liturgy is, consequently, the celebration not only of the human experience, but of the new humanity, the life of the new age that is revealed, embodied, and anticipated in Jesus Christ. Liturgy is, consequently, not merely a way of fitting in with the universe as we find it, but a way of becoming what we believe we and it must be. It is therefore educational (in the etymological sense of *educare,* to lead out) but primarily at the level of metaphor and intuition rather than at the level of rationalized concept.

The New Testament throws light on this educational aspect of liturgy, although somewhat negatively. Both Paul and James dealt roughly with congregations that allowed patterns of behavior to develop that distorted the authentic substance of the liturgy. Paul wrote to the Corinthians, in 1 Corinthians 11:17, 20-22:

> I do not commend you, because when you come together it
> is not for the better but for the worse. . . . When you meet
> together, it is not the Lord's supper that you eat. For in
> eating, each one goes ahead with his own meal, and one is

hungry and another is drunk. What! Do you not have houses to eat and drink in? Or do you despise the church of God and humiliate those who have nothing?

Underlying Paul's outrage is a sense of the liturgical assembly as the model of the new age; it is, consequently, both the testing ground of Christian integrity and the schoolhouse of the "kingdom of God." This sense is even stronger in James 2:1-9:

> My brethren, show no partiality as you hold the faith of our Lord Jesus Christ, the Lord of glory. For if a man with gold rings and in fine clothing comes into your assembly, and a poor man in shabby clothing also comes in, and you pay attention to the one who wears the fine clothing and say, "Have a seat here, please," while you say to the poor man, "Stand there," or "Sit at my feet," have you not made distinctions among yourselves, and become judges with evil thoughts? Has not God chosen those who are poor in the world to be rich in faith and heirs of the kingdom which he has promised to those who love him? But you have dishonored the poor man. Is it not the rich who oppress you, is it not they who drag you into court? Is it not they who blaspheme that honorable name by which you are called?
>
> If you really fulfil the royal law, according to the scripture, "You shall love your neighbor as yourself," you do well. But if you show partiality, you commit sin.

For James, the liturgy is to be a microcosm of God's own justice, the justice in which God stands with and for the oppressed. Personal spirituality is not so much the route to that justice (as in the principle, "when people are converted in their hearts they will do good"); it is its expression.

Christian liturgy is about the wholeness and integration of people and their world. If it allows a distinction between individual and group, it is a dialectical distinction in which the health of each depends entirely on the primacy of the other in its eyes and the reign of God stands beyond both.

The liturgical assembly either reflects social justice and care for the person or it mocks the Christ.

This introduces a final principle, which may best be expressed in the form of a question: Who owns the liturgy? This is not a juridical question; it does not refer to the control of liturgy within a given polity, whether by bishop or session or prayer book. It refers to the dynamics of the liturgical assembly, to the texture of relationships that are (or are not) expressed when a congregation gathers for its typical acts.

The tendency in all organizations is for leadership roles to be first institutionalized and then sacralized. Religious organizations find it difficult to resist or reverse this tendency. Once sacralized, leadership roles tend to arrogate to themselves certain activities of the organization. Liturgical activities, which are already sacral in quality, are ripe candidates for this process. (A parallel process may be observed in the medical world in the struggle between physicians and midwives.) Much of the history of liturgy is a story of clericalization punctuated by resistance movements.

The question is not whether leadership is appropriate, but whether it subverts or enables the right of a congregation of Christians to enjoy a sense of common partnership in liturgy. Liturgical leadership is not exempt from the conditions required by Jesus, in Matthew 20:25-27:

> You know that the rulers of the Gentiles lord it over them, and their great men exercise authority over them. It shall not be so among you; but whoever would be great among you must be your servant, and whoever would be first among you must be your slave.

It is almost impossible to meet these conditions in a liturgy in which one person is the principal actor in virtually all roles, in which the various aspects of a complex activity are not shared, in which the organic life of the Christian body is not visible. The application of Jesus' conditions to the conduct of liturgy is essential precisely because liturgy is, as we have seen, the mirror and schoolhouse of God's reign, and the abrogation of individual power in favor of the shared power of mutual service is a condition (if not *the* condition) of living within God's reign.

Some Applications to the Small Congregation

All these principles are available to small congregations, and some may be realized more immediately and concretely in such settings. The very compactness of a small congregation ought to make it more difficult to abstract and then compartmentalize the various elements of parish life from their center in its liturgy: The mission of the church should be seen to be the actualization of the vision these people share; the educational program of the church should find its source and much of its expression in the weekly liturgical assembly. A host of subcommittees devoted to these and other concerns is less necessary in a small congregation that takes its liturgy seriously.

The condition of intentionality is a large one. Too often in churches with formal liturgical traditions, intentionality is abandoned in favor of reliance on the established texts and gestures. And the false assumption that large is normative casts a heavy shadow over the self-confidence of the small, sometimes resulting in meanness of spirit and sometimes in a frantic and unsuccessful attempt to imitate the standards of the large (this is particularly unfortunate in the area of music).

A fundamental task for leaders of small congregations is to persuade the congregation to become intentional about its liturgy. This usually involves the formation of a liturgy committee, but this committee must be an informed liturgy committee. People need to discover a hermeneutical approach to their liturgical tradition, to determine for themselves how the tradition got to be like it is, and to identify elements in their own life experience that throw light back onto the tradition and its origins, a light which allows them to see how to rework the tradition for their own day.

No congregation is too small to have a group of people meet every week to discuss and plan the liturgy. Ministers as well as congregational leaders who work with them should look on this engagement in liturgy as an art form. In terms of anthropological history, liturgy is the source of all the arts: dance, painting, storytelling, music, mime, drama—all of them were spun out of the rites and myths of prehistoric humanity. The purpose of an art form is not to tell people what to think and do (that is propaganda); it is to so present the symbolized insights of the tradition (what we Christians call revelation) that the participants will, through their own insight, discover these riches afresh for themselves.

This task is not beyond the resources of the smallest of congregations or the abilities of the simplest of people. Society is full of unexpressed, undetected, unowned, unknown folk wisdom (what a waste!). Intention is required in order to make the theme of the day (whether expressed in lectionary readings or selected in some other way) available to the assembly; this involves imagination and humility.

In the small congregation it is vital that a decision be made for participation rather than performance, i.e., to so structure and plan the liturgy that the whole congregation and each person within it will be conscious of engagement in common acts. This does not mean that everyone must do the same thing at the same time, nor does it mean that some people will not assume more prominent leadership roles than others. This does not even mean that there is no place for performance, e.g., a musical solo, a choir anthem. It does mean that performance should not be regarded as a necessary end in itself, but simply as another expression of participation in an organic and variegated whole. The liturgy should not be treated as if it were something inert that needed decorating to liven it up; the liturgy—the active proclamation of scripture with commentary and prayer of deep concern in a setting of hymns and song, and the thankful telling of the salvation story over bread and wine, which are eaten and drunk—is a living thing that demands the serious involvement of each individual and of the community as a whole.

The minister and other congregational leaders who form the liturgy committee should attempt to ensure the active involvement in leadership roles of members of the congregation who represent not only the lay order, but the actual mixture of age-groups, racial groups, sexes, etc. of which the congregation is composed. In a small congregation it may be impossible—or undesirable—to arrange for all subgroupings to be represented at each liturgy; however, a congregation in which the young or the old or women or black people never emerge as visible leaders of liturgy will ultimately fail to discover itself as the people of God.

How a small congregation uses music and space may be the best way to measure its freedom from big-church mentality. A small congregation whose choir and organist struggle with only limited or minimal success to produce performance music intended for musicians of professional standard has not come to terms with its own reality. This failure is a particular tragedy in an era in which probably more composers are producing more music—much of it good and much of it intended for participation—than at any other time in the church's history. Similarly, a church building which is jammed with every piece of furniture that might be required in the spacious setting of a great cathedral and in which worshipers are isolated from one another by the arrangement of pews, pulpit, choir loft, and other furnishings suggests a congregation which has not discovered the enormous potential that lies in the intimacy its size allows.

Reflections on a Radical Alternative

We cannot address the subject of small congregations today without reference to one of the extraordinary phenomena of our time: the basic Christian communities that have appeared in Brazil and in third-world areas.[3] These basic Christian communities are small congregations, but with a difference that provides a critical standard for our evaluation of what we think is the norm.

These basic Christian communities have an improbable pedigree; they are a declericalized movement brought into being and turned free, more or less, by a clericalized church. They are a post-Vatican II expression of the church's solidarity with the poor in a highly polarized society, as well as a response of the bishops to a critical shortage of clergy. They are also the new flowering of movements that preceded them—liturgical, lay, biblical, and theological.

The important point about the basic Christian communities is that they throw on the people who belong to them the responsibility to discover how to be the church in their own way. Such communities may be established by traveling priests, nuns, or lay evangelists, but after that start their leadership is internal.

Slavish imitation of the model of basic Christian communities in first-world cultures is unlikely to be creative. The model is clearly dependent on the need for third-world people to discover and name and own their social worthlessness, their exile from their own society and its benefits. The exile of first-world people is more complex, partly because they (albeit unwittingly) are the cause rather than the recipients of much of the world's suffering and oppression and partly because the world of affluence has inner distortions and oppressions of its own. However, the underlying principles of the model remain valid for all small congregations: Liturgy is not a process for checking out of the world, but a means of checking into a world of mutual support and social change, and this process is facilitated by intimacy and honesty as well as by common analysis and confrontation of the systemic roots of alienation.

First-world small congregations and third-world basic Christian communities are, in some ways, reverse images of each other. The former are often made up of like-*minded* people who come together to liturgies that reinforce their attitudes; in the latter there tend to be like-*status* people whose liturgies change their world view and their capacity for effecting change. Many first-world congregations need to discover the dynamics of the other model.

What Can Judicatory Officers Do to Help Small Congregations?

First, judicatory officers can help small congregations by stressing the corporate nature of the congregation and the need for this nature to be expressed in liturgy. Almost every contact with a congregation should be regarded as an opportunity to make the point that it is responsible for its own symbolic life and that responsibility includes being enlightened and informed. A passive maintenance of unconsidered tradition will, in the long run, erode a congregation's spirit. It is up to the members of the congregation to be sensitive to cultural change and to the needs of newcomers and young people; they should not wait for a minister to impose new liturgy on them.

Second, judicatory officers should also stress that the minister is a leader within a corporate action rather than a performer before an audience. They need to ask themselves: "Does this denomination reward stars? Are top performers most likely to make it to the big steeples, and if so, what does that say about supportive and enabling forms of ministry?" (Indeed, what does it say about Jesus' notions of ministry?) A "star" system will, inevitably, work to the detriment of small-congregation liturgy. Are remuneration scales unjustly linked to a career system that encourages prima donna leadership styles? What can the denomination do about this?

Third, judicatory officers should make sure that regional (diocesan, conference, etc.) liturgy committees give proportionate time and attention to the needs of small congregations. Someone on the committee should be constantly on the lookout for materials—journals, handbooks, new music, etc.—that will help liturgy leaders in small congregations. There should be a regional newsletter and a distribution system.

Fourth, these officers can also help small congregations by encouraging the formation of liturgy committees (however small the congregation) and by providing training opportunities for their leaders, e.g., workshops, correspondence courses, tapes, reading lists.[6]

Fifth, they should provide regular liturgy workshops for mixed groups of ministers and laypeople, who need to work together to become sensitive to the human dynamics of liturgy as well as to tell each other what helps (or does not help) them most. Workshop settings sometimes provide an opportunity for the discovery of community and the corporate nature of liturgy when these essential elements have been locked out of ordinary congregational life by time, familiarity, and institutionalization.

Finally, all regional liturgical occasions (ordinations, synod and conference services) should model carefully planned liturgy that is within the capability of small congregations in terms of music, style, and lay involvement. Good liturgy is not taught; it is modeled. Elaborate and triumphalist services have, in the long run, a negative effect.

Postscript

At this point we arrive where we started: Small congregations have the advantage in doing liturgy, in enabling people to move from the symbolic into that worship which is the purpose and fulfillment of human life. No one may expect that movement to be automatic, yet an element of evaluation may be introduced: Does our liturgy speak to our yearnings for that worship in terms sufficiently concrete to be imagined? Or does it transfer us from the real present into an unreal future?

We have already noted Irenaeus' words, that "the glory of God is humanity fully alive"; the second half of that aphorism is seldom quoted: "Thus the life of humanity is the vision of God." The implications of this statement are profound and simple, obvious and elusive: The pursuit of the "wholly other" ends in discovering ourselves, transformed and transfigured, fully alive. The purpose of liturgy is not to force that discovery or to claim it prematurely; the purpose of liturgy is to anticipate, to see the end in the beginning, and thus to illuminate "the way" (that most ancient name of the church). Because the focus of the exercise is people and their most basic symbols, this microcosm of humanity that stands for all the possibility and destiny of all the rest, their number on any given occasion is unimportant.

3

The Art of Pastoring a Small Congregation

Carl S. Dudley

As a preface to my comments on leadership of small churches, I must make two important and controversial assumptions that provide the foundations for my approach; these assumptions have been discussed at length in other contexts. First, I assume that the small congregation is a single-cell, primary group that carries the socioreligious culture of its members and constituency.[1] Second, I assume a difference exists between the science of management and the art of leadership. Management skills can be learned, but leadership is discovered in relationship to a group who confirm the leader with particular authority. Pastoral leadership always implies and accepts a spiritual dimension, a priestly role.[2] The power of the pastor stems from the pastor's willingness to walk with the congregation through the abyss, through the mysteries of life. This art of leadership takes on unique dimensions within the intimacy of a small congregation.

Small-church pastors do not need to fit any mold or image of the "perfect type." They, like the members of the congregations they serve, come in all sorts and sizes of body and psyche. But leaders of these congregations need to appreciate the dynamics of small congregations; they need to honor the strengths that make the small church so durable. As a *sampler* of what this means, I have noted ten characteristics of small congregations that establish some perimeters for constructive pastoral leadership.

1. Small Congregations Have a Strong People-Concern

"How are you?" is a question, not just a greeting. I learned this from an elder of the congregation. He was well known in the community as a manager, and I thought I had the perfect managerial job for him in the congregation. The next time that I met him, I immediately launched into a description of his new "opportunity" in the church. He let me talk for several minutes before he gently stopped me: "Reverend, how is your wife? Is she feeling well today?" For him, this was not an interruption, but rather the only place to begin. He had not heard anything until we took time to find out how everyone was feeling that day.

That question is a revelation. It suggests the powerful, personal commitments that support most social ministries in small congregations. When I ask congregations to tell me about their social ministries they go blank. "What's that?" But when I ask about their care for others they frequently have extensive, personal ways of looking after the people who are hurting. They will mobilize a ministry the minute they know "one of ours is hurting." A large congregation might have a committee to study the county and recommend a program for the most important problem of the area. A small congregation responds first and organizes the committee later, maybe. The pastor who cares about social ministry must focus not on "problems," but on people who are hurting.

"How are you?" When this question is asked by the small-church pastor it should serve a dual purpose, inquiring into both body and soul. It does not need to be heavy or awkward. But "our pastor" is expected to care about both.

2. Small-church Worship Is a Folk Dance

We can see it when we make a drawing of the sanctuary and put the worshipers in their regular places. Most people sit in the same pews every Sunday. As a matter of fact, they enter the sanctuary at the same time and move through the same patterns. Worship has a rhythm that is as carefully choreographed as any dance routine on Broadway. You can set your watch by the entrances and take attendance by the empty places. Not everyone sits in exactly the same place every time, but even those who move about have "gone visiting." They may not be able to say why they moved, but often they can say who they sat with the last time in that place. Worship location is a social experience.

One pastor I worked with had been serving his church for seventeen years. One Sunday, after all were settled, he invited everyone to "worship from a new perspective" by changing seats for the occasion. Although this happened several years ago, that congregation is still talking about the time the pastor "messed up worship."

The art of pastoring is making the most of the natural rhythm of the congregation. Pastors who urge the members to "come down front so we can have a sense of community" do not understand the accumulated history of the people in that place. Sensitive pastors can find the rhythm and learn the tune. Pastors can make the tune happy or sad, can be inviting or inhibiting, can fight it or go with the flow. They are like fiddlers of the worship, who take a well-known tune and help the people want to dance.

[48]

3. Small Churches Trust Face-to-face Information

The small church is a network of people who have known one another in many ways for many years. There is an established pattern for disseminating information. It is nicely called the grapevine and unkindly called the gossip mill. In a large church a newsletter is essential to relay important information to the membership. In a small church the membership knows most of the important stuff already; in this case, the purpose of the newsletter is to clarify a few forgotten facts. But the significant "stuff" must happen face to face.

Sometimes the caring network seems to be a barrier to progress. Planning in the small church has been described as two hours of small talk, followed by five minutes of deciding "we will do it again, just like last year." To the pastor who has just arrived or to a member who has recently joined the congregation and has a shiny new idea, the network is a nuisance. Newcomers often hope to find a place for themselves by suggesting some new program or approach. But even if they remain silent, they do not know the central figures of the small talk.

In a meeting of a small-church board the chairperson for building and grounds presented a report on fixing the roof, complete with bids from three local contractors. After he made his formal report another board member commented that old Smitty had fixed the roof the last time it needed to be repaired. Someone else offered the opinion that Mr. Smith was too old and added that Mr. Smith's daughter had moved to California. Next came the information that her baby was ill. Another person said, "In the hospital." The board members seemed more interested in Smitty's granddaughter than in repairing the roof. They were running out one more strand of the network of relationships that holds the church together.

The pastor must be a listener in the grapevine, not a participant. The art of pastoring includes the gift of patience until the pieces of the network begin to form a large tapestry of kind and caring people. The pastor must raise up this quality of caring in preaching, prayers, and pastoral visits, because often the congregation is more Christian than it dares to admit to itself.

4. In the Small Church a New Member Must Join the Past

In a large congregation a new member can earn the right to belong. Most evangelism materials urge congregations to set up future-oriented groups, with a common interest and a mutual task. You can join such groups by wiping out your past and sharing your gifts for a common future. But the small, culture-carrying congregation is different. New members must join the past and find a place in the social network. This is the difference between conversion and adoption.

In one congregation I served, a widow who had been absent for several weeks returned to discover a young couple had taken up residence in "her pew." On the following Sunday she arrived early enough to meet the couple and invite them to sit with her. After worship she told them what that pew meant to her. It had been "her pew" for thirty-eight years; she had seen her children grow up in that pew and vividly remembered sharing it with her husband. As they sat together in "her pew," she told the couple about the church. Then something strange happened. The couple became part of the congregation. They took up residence in the pew behind hers for as long as they remained. They were family members when they heard and appreciated her history and when she gave them a place of their own.

The art of pastoring includes helping older members remember their history and helping newcomers find a place in the fabric and flow of the congregation. Membership cannot be earned, for many active members (and pastors) are still outsiders after years of trying. Membership must be given by adoption, where both parties honor the past and celebrate each other in the present. A church that does not like itself has no room for new members.

5. Small Congregations Live on "People Time"

Some pastors seem to be trained better as managers and administrators and believe they can measure the effectiveness of ministry by the number of new programs they initiate. Before I visit a congregation I usually ask the pastor about the church and hear a litany of program activities. But when I sit down with the members they tell me about relationships among the members.

I asked one member why he was always late to every activity. He replied that he was never late, because, he said, "I live on people-time: It begins when I arrive and lasts as long as I can remember it." Members of small churches participate emotionally in whatever happens in the church. They want events that are worth remembering. Even if they do not attend, they want to hear about them and they want to tell others. They live on people-time.

Some pastors are program pushers, with a different program for every age-group in the congregation. This push is exhausting for the small church, where everyone emotionally attends everything that happens at church. One denominational executive told me he could predict how long it would take a congregation to get organized to call a pastor after the previous pastor left. He said it was in direct proportion to the number of new programs the departing pastor had initiated. "The more programs, the longer the time of transition." He added that the congregation is exhausted and needs time for rest and recovery.

Small churches live on people-time. The art of pastoring includes shaping fewer activities of greater significance—making events worth talking about.

6. Many Small Churches Use Conflict for Catharsis

Pastors who have been taught to manage conflict often find small churches baffling. Small churches often do not manage conflict well. They fight.

Many studies of small groups have suggested that conflict in extended-family settings is a kind of affirmation. Members are free to release their emotions—affection as well as anger. Like children home from school in the bosom of the family, members of small congregations squabble to prove that there is something more that holds them together. Fighting is an affirmation of a bond that is bigger than all the contestants.

In a settled small church many members' roles have been etched into the dynamics of the congregation through years of repetition. In order for such a large "small group" to hold itself together some members have an unspoken agreement not to exhaust the others by their affection. Conflict is often stylized. When a new proposal is presented, if the red team is in favor, the blue team is opposed and the green team will not play. The conflict may serve the same cathartic function for the congregation as spectator sports do for larger populations. Everyone feels involved when the conflict happens and feels better when it is over.

Frequently, young men and women return to the seminary with sad stories of disaster regarding their serving as pastors of small churches. They tell of introducing a new idea, which caused a fight. They lament: "Look what a terrible thing I have done." We at the seminary gently tell them that such guilt is nonsense, because the new pastor is never that important. If they will inquire carefully, they will discover that the same people who started the conflict also kept the pot boiling, stood on the sidelines and cheered, and will finally put on the lid when things have gone far enough. Conflict can be serious when people are getting hurt. But sometimes the pastor needs to expose and enjoy the game, not elevate it into a cosmic conflict of terrible consequence. All conflict should be challenged; some should be stopped. Much of the conflict in small churches can be revealing and, in the bosom of Christ, can be fun.

7. Small Congregations Are the Carriers of History

The place of worship can be a kind of cocoon that protects memories from the erosion of time. The rhythm is not only weekly events, but a sense of the changing seasons that bring an extended family together. Typically, the small church is larger than its membership, embracing many vicarious "members" who live in the shadow of the steeple or whose family members belong to the congregation.

Annual events provide a kind of accordionlike, expanded involvement for many people who are not official members but share in the ministry of the congregation. Because these events are usually centered in the semisecular life of the congregation, they are often opposed by the most recent pastor. But they will happen anyway, organized by annual officers and attended by annual members. Annual events have been described as "what the last pastor was opposed to, which is why he is the last pastor."

This seasonal rhythm of history has two important implications for leadership: First, it provides a resource for ministry that is much larger than the membership. Second, it provides the leverage for change.

Annual events are times when the whole Christian community gathers for celebration. They may be either planned, as the Christmas Eve candlelight singing or the Fall Harvest

[53]

Festival, or unplanned, as in the death of a church saint or the marriage of a favorite daughter or son. But they are marked by the return and receptivity of many marginal members of the extended family. When these events are used to interpret the story of the congregation as an engaging ministry, "in the future as we have in the past," a large number of persons who are not official members will support and even join the effort. The sensitive pastor knows how to make the most of annual events, a birthday party (Pentecost) for the extended family. Annual events help the larger congregation renew its identity.

A sense of history provides a leverage for change. Beware of old victories, because the great moments get better every time they are repeated and sometimes make the present effort seem less significant. The valleys of history may be helpful, because "we did it then and we can do it again." But most helpful for change are the older historians, who carry the images of the congregation's history.

Many pastors emphasize creativity, which suggests that the vision came ex nihilo, out of nothing. But in a culture-carrying congregation the strongest emotion is anchored in the imagination, the images of the congregation. Every congregation has its storytellers. I served a church that had a Stuffers Club, which put out the mail once a month. The members of this club explained that they were late middle-aged, with a minimum age limit of seventy-five to belong. They had stories about everyone for all occasions. Further, the Stuffers had outlived status; they treated everyone as somebody's child. And they knew that anyone who said, "We have always done it this way," was lying.

When we wanted to change things we talked it over with the Stuffers Club. After chewing on the suggestion for a time the Stuffers could invariably find precedent: "That sounds like the way we used to do it with old Reverend Pierson." When they had decided that it was history there was no one to argue with them—who else had been there? Further, they had a special determination to see that it happened. If we had a problem with the mere officers of the church, the Stuffers Club always found a way to help the members see the light. This club is especially supportive of young pastors. Historical imagination offers the culture-carrying church a world of options for change and a tremendous release of energy to see it through. Pastoral leadership uses history as a resource for change to meet the present challenge of the congregation.

8. Small Churches Want to Be Part of Denominations as an Extension of the Family

Most small churches know that they are parochial and need a larger vision. They are not blind to the changes that surround them or to the needs of distant Christians. But they want to be included in the denominational family, and too often they have been just another statistic in the denominational annual report.

To be part of the denomination, small-church members need to hear the "good stuff" by way of the friendly grapevine, not the printed page. They need to feel that they are sufficiently significant to be told personally about the latest program materials and the most recent resignations. They need a denomination that takes worship as seriously as debating the issues and promoting the program.

For the church to feel included in the denomination, someone must visit the congregation's annual events without a sense of obligation. At one such annual event I heard an executive tell a funny (although risqué) story about one of the staid, old patriarchs of the congregation. The story was a bit touchy, but the congregation loved it. The executive was one of the family, and the congregation felt its acceptance by the larger denomination.

Too often money alienates the small church from the denomination. If the church is broke, it feels second-rate. If the denomination provides mission support, the church feels patronized. Frequently, a pastor feels the brunt of ambivalence that is aimed at the denomination but deflected to hit the convenient target: the local clergy. In my experience, a congregation is much healthier when it knows it is paying for its own ministry, even if this means less than a full-time pastor. The problems of financing as they affect leadership are too complex to be unpacked here and too important to be ignored.

9. Small Churches Have Access and Influence Disproportionate to Their Size

Small-church pastors are known in the community, and often the members of small churches permeate various community structures. Some pastors develop a community image and use it to good advantage.

Small congregations have an ingenious way of making the pastors into characters. The members tell stories about the times the pastor goofed. I remember dropping the ring at a wedding, when it was caught in the bride's dress and three of us could not find it. In a large church the members might snicker, but who would they tell? In a small church everyone knows. Once I said the wrong name at a funeral and "buried" the person's brother. By morning everyone knew. Another time, after surviving a terrible service of the Lord's Supper, I sought solace by taking communion to the shut-in members. But they all knew already and asked me to tell them, "Was it really that bad this morning, pastor?"

To the polished, professional pastor such stories are offensive. But to the small church these tales are a way of developing character. To the characters—the pastors with good stories—they will turn in times of trouble.

When the whole community tells stories about the small-church pastor, he or she has become a parson among those people. The parson has access to the full range of community people. There is no home or office where the parson is unwelcome and no question that the parson cannot ask. To be made a parson for a community takes at least five years. Whereas the large-church pastor may build an empire from programs, the small-church pastor can build a community from earthy trust and human weakness.

10. The Small Church Is a Way of Thinking About Relationships

The small church is the right size, so that everyone feels as though they know everyone else, and they want to know all there is to know about the pastor. Studies of career patterns for clergy indicate that some pastors are specialists, some are organizers, some are counselors, and some are generalists. But small-church members want a lover. They want someone who will call them by name, who walks with them through the uncertainties and transitions of life, who always picks up where they left off, even after weeks or months of absence. They want someone who understands.

What is your reaction as a pastor or as a listening layperson to the sweet, elderly person who sleeps through the sermon and then tells the pastor, "That was a wonderful message!"? Sometimes there is the urge to challenge the person's integrity or at least to ignore his or her impoliteness. But the pastor who is in the small-church mode will embrace the parishioner and say, "I love you too." The pastor tries to get inside the values of the members as much as the parishioner has valued the priorities of the pastor.

In an overorganized and underhumanized world the small church is a way of thinking and feeling about people who want to be understood in their character and in their kinkiness. They want a pastor who will call them by name and by nicknames, whose body space is invadable, and about whom they have good stories. They want a lover.

The art of pastoring a small congregation depends on venturing beyond the safety of organizational props into the uncertainties of walking with people who need God's help just as we do. In loving, the risk is great, but the reward is immeasurable.

4

The Ethnic/Minority
Small-church Pastor

Emmanuel L. McCall

GEORGE BERNARD SHAW is reported to have said, "The only person who behaves sensibly towards me is my tailor, for each time we meet, he measures me anew. While all the rest continue with their old measurements of me assuming that they will do, my tailor measures me anew each time we meet."

This quote has immediate application for the *ethnic small-church* pastor. It involves the measurements and value judgments that are directed toward him* by himself, his peers, his congregation, the majority community, the ethnic community, and his family. Some see ethnicity as a negative factor. Others see the *small* church as a liability.

The purpose of this chapter is to examine the value judgments—measurements, if you please—that impinge on the ethnic small-church pastor. In some instances alterations of our value judgments are necessary. In other instances the skills of new tailors are required.

*The use of male references in this chapter reflects the reality that nearly all ethnic/minority pastors are male.

Pastoring an Ethnic Small Church Has Some Advantages

One of the most decided advantages of pastoring an ethnic small church is the community leadership status available to the ethnic pastor. This status is not automatic. It should not be universally assumed. It is *available* primarily because of the role that the pastor plays in his congregation. As a leader in his community, the pastor can utilize a wider berth of platforms for the exercise of ministry. These platforms may come through educational situations, civic concerns, economics, crisis events, political action, or community needs. He therefore translates his ministry into what he can accomplish for members of the ethnic community through his involvement in these wider concerns rather than just through the immediate church fellowship.

This wider berth is necessary for the ethnic pastor because his ministry, by virtue of the circumstances surrounding America's stigmas of ethnicity, requires him to be the advocate and ombudsman for his community. His "priestly" function extends beyond the walls of the church house and the boundaries of the community.

A certain amount of prestige goes with this advocacy role. To be sure, the prestige of the ethnic pastor will be the source of irritation to some in both the minority and the majority communities. Some will perceive him as a troublemaker. His own folk may call him an opportunist. If the pastor seeks to serve rather than to be self-serving, he can overcome and outlive his detractors by the results of his ministry.

As a community leader, a serving pastor seeks to make full use of the skills of other ethnic members. He encourages them for the good of the whole as well as the needs of the ethnic community. In doing so he multiplies his ministry, removes the need for his personal involvement in multiple activities, and helps those persons find larger fulfillment.

A second advantage the ethnic small-church pastor has is that he gets to know his members in ways that are more difficult for the pastor of a larger congregation. The small congregation allows the possibility of his influence to be felt. This influence should facilitate fellowship and ministry and offer a more immediate opportunity for crisis response. By only having to concentrate on a small number of people, the conscientious pastor is able to do some planned discipling. If this discipling is consistent with New Testament principles, the well-being of the church and the community will be enhanced and the pastor's ministry multiplied.

A third advantage the ethnic small-church pastor has is the time available for study, family, and recreation. Some variables may negate this observation. Such variables include whether or not the pastor is bivocational and whether there are persons who can be trained to give leadership to other ministries the pastor is called on to fulfill. These controlling variables also include the availability of financial, study, and recreational resources. The extent to which the small church enables one to enjoy these leisures is dependent on individual responses to the challenges elaborated in the next section.

The Challenges for the Ethnic Small-church Pastor

To be sure, some problems of the small-church pastor are compounded by his ethnicity.

1. Unless his denomination has a subsidy program, he must subscribe to a substandard life-style or become bivocational of necessity, or his wife *must* work to supplement their income. The problem is compounded if the other vocation is not prestigious or if it is demeaning, i.e., if the pastor works as a janitor or yardsman or his wife works as a maid. Such a situation not only lowers the personal self-esteem of both the

pastor and his wife but diminishes them in the eyes of the majority and minority communities.

Because of the duality of his roles, the bivocational pastor also suffers personal fatigue. His family life suffers, his personal and family time is diminished, thus producing a variety of other problems. These problems may cause him to harbor feelings of resentment toward fellow pastors in better situations, to bide his time until something better comes along, or to fail to offer his own congregation the best that is needed for their growth and fulfillment as well as his own.

2. Another challenge the ethnic small-church pastor faces is conditioned by the circumstances of his educational preparation. If he attended Anglo-oriented institutions and lacked the skills and resources for transposing his training to his own ethnic identity, he might easily have "anglocized" himself out of his community. Some illustrate this as "oreo"-ing (blacks) or "apple"-ing (native American). Essentially, this means that the person has lost his indigenous orientation and is therefore less capable of being a leader in the congregation and in the community.

3. A third challenge for the ethnic small-church pastor is to adapt the denominational literature and resources written for the larger community to the needs of his group. The crisis is that (aside from the language) his ethnic group may use words, concepts, ideas, and interpolations that are different from those of the larger community. Thus, the pastor must reconstruct (blackenize) these denominational resources so they can benefit his congregation. One pastor likens this challenge to eating fish. In his family, some prefer the tail, some want only the fillets, some prefer the head. Each has the privilege of claiming that which is individually useful and discarding or giving away the remains. A similar

process must be employed by ethnics using literature and resources that are not adapted to their needs.

4. Some ethnic small-church pastors are challenged by the historical realities of that denomination's history. I can better illustrate this from the black experience. Most blacks who are religious are Baptists (47 percent). Their rootage is in Baptist life as experienced in the South. This experience was related to the Great Awakening experiences of the 1700s and 1800s. These experiences emphasized experiential religion over intellect. Consequently, black Baptist churches and pastors have had to wrestle with the concerns of less academic pulpits and emotionally expectant congregations. As more and more laypeople receive better educations, the communication gap between pulpit and pew widens. The domineering emphasis on the experiential aspects of faith has overshadowed the development of the indigenous resources needed to respond to the congregation's growing demands.

5. A fifth challenge to the ethnic small-church pastor is that his and his group's needs are not taken seriously by the majority community. He and his group become appendages that could just as well be discarded. They are tolerated but not loved or valued for their own intrinsic worth. They are seldom understood and frequently misunderstood. They are the objects of ethnic jokes and sick humor. At denominational meetings they are lonely and isolated because of the lack of bonding elements (race, college or seminary ties, social groups) that give cohesion to others. In larger gatherings their skills are either not used or, at best, are underused. If they are not bilingual, they lack an awareness and appreciation for the transactions that seem to excite others. Consequently, they miss the enjoyment of inspiration and

fellowship. It is convenient for the ethnic small-church pastor to remain at home during such "great" ecclesiastical gatherings.

6. Because he is a leader in his community, the ethnic small-church pastor must give unusual amounts of time to the *total* needs of his group. Such needs may take the form of fighting racial, social, and economic injustice or may mean interpreting the particular concerns of his group to the majority community or interpreting the larger group's reactions to his group. He may have to serve as his group's ombudsman. It may be necessary for him to deal with his group's customs or traditions that are in conflict with their own best interests.

Until such time as he can develop lay leaders to provide these services, the ethnic small-church pastor is burdened with these responsibilities.

Some Options Toward Resolution

What can we as denominational leaders do in response to such challenges? The first thing we must not do is act as if the ethnic/minority small-church pastor were not there or will just go away. If left unanswered, the ethnic small-church pastor and his congregation will feel kinship only with those who share his concerns. This may lead to ethnic caucuses or defection to other religious groupings. At best, the group might remain small, immobile, and ineffective.

I suggest consideration be given to the following alternatives.

1. College and seminary faculties and denominational leaders *must* be helped to become sensitive to the particular needs of non-Anglos in their midst. "Making them like us" is an irresponsible response. Equipping ethnic persons to

[64]

indigenize their academic experiences will return them to the ethnic community better able *to minister, not mimic.* America is not an ethnic melting pot; it is a stewpot. Every culture and race should be valued for its own inherent worth, while contributing to the good of the whole.

2. Denominational publishers should make concerted efforts to include ethnic consultants and writers in their production processes and to see to it that resources are provided in the idiom of particular groups. Ethnic representation in artwork and photos helps the "out" groups feel "in."

3. Every opportunity must be taken to sensitize the majority community with an awareness of its ethnic constituents. The ethnic small-church pastor can be spared additional burdens if the majority community understands how its actions or inactions contribute to particular problems faced by ethnic minorities.

4. Conferences, retreats, and training sessions should be made available to ethnic small-church pastors, their wives, and lay leaders and should be planned in response to *their* needs, concerns, and priorities. Such assemblies must be *theirs* and must utilize persons and techniques that best communicate with them.

5. An option that is only in the exploratory stages but that has infinite possibilities is being developed by the Redford School of Theology of Southwest Baptist College, Bolivar, Missouri. Dean Charles Chaney recognizes the denominational growth potential of small churches. Because these churches are often pastored by men who, of necessity, are bivocational, Chaney is proposing an academic program that responds to the particular needs of the small-church pastor and gives special attention to ethnic small-church pastors.

He further proposes trade schools that will provide training in "honorable" professions, so their graduates simultaneously receive vocational and theological training. This option deserves a chance to prove its worth. Its potential may make the small church more attractive than ever before.

In Conclusion

The ethnic small church is here to stay. *It will be pastored.* How and under what circumstances largely depend on the creative, Spirit-led actions of the majority and ethnic/minority communities. As someone has wisely observed, "We may have come over to this country on different ships, but we are in the same boat now." We can strive for mutual survival or perish as fools. How we tailor the future is one aspect of the resolution of the problem.

The only person who behaves sensibly towards me is my tailor, for each time we meet, he measures me anew. While all the rest continue with their old measurements of me assuming that they will do, my tailor measures me anew each time we meet.

5

Women in Ministry in the Small Congregation

Lynne Josselyn

IN THE UNITED METHODIST church I served some years ago, there was no baptismal font; instead, a small silver bowl—not sterling, just a small silver bowl—was used. Also in this church the two young boys who served as acolytes always processed during the first hymn. One carried a taper to light the candles and the other carried the bowl when there was to be a baptism. One memorable Sunday, as the first hymn ended, the boys took their places in the front pew and I took my place in the chancel area. Then we all sat down—one of us to considerable dismay. During the hymn one of the boys, struggling to hold his hymnbook and the bowl filled with water, resolved the struggle by placing the bowl in the pew. At the end of the hymn, forgetting how he had resolved his difficulty, he sat down—right in the bowl! Poor boy. Not only did he have wet pants, but worse than that, we had no water to baptize the baby. And what was he going to do about that? Finally, he left (wet pants and all) to refill the bowl.

Small-church adventures—how wonderful they are, especially when we are part of them. In the close fellowship of the small church *everyone* knows about the adventures and shares in remembering them. Sometimes the recalling is vivid to us. In one small church where I served communion the folks would come to the altar rail to receive. This is not unusual, except that in this church there were no little holes in the altar rail to hold the empty glasses, so somehow we had to collect all the glasses after the people had drunk their juice. I carried a tray—partly full and partly empty—down the row of communicants so each could place his or her glass on the tray. But one woman who put her glass on the tray had a heavier hand than I did. She upset the whole thing all over me and all over her. There were glasses everywhere. The junior choir thought it a marvelous scene to behold. My white stole still has a stain from the grape juice spilled at the Mars Hill United Methodist Church (Maine).

When I was asked to write about how to provide support for women in ministry in small congregations, I thought first about my own experiences—of an empty baptismal bowl and spilled grape juice. These memories and many more from the small churches where I have served speak of the joy and struggle of humans, women and men seeking to be the church. So, first of all, I want to share out of my own experience.

Two key words are important to me, as they were to the entire group that gathered in Detroit, in March 1982, to face leadership issues in small congregations: effective and support. When it comes to ministry I believe these two words are inherently related. No one can be *effective* in ministry for long without *support*. Effective means actual—not merely theoretical, but making a striking impression. When someone says, "That was an effective sermon," she or he means that that sermon made an impression. When you are described by your church board as being an effective pastor, you know you have made an impression—a striking impression—on at least one person. One can hardly be effective again and again without support. Support is how we survive to be effective. Support means to give courage of faith to, to help, to comfort, to uphold, to carry or bear the weight of. The support we receive enables us to continue to be effective.

We cannot survive in ministry alone—none of us. Even Jesus was not in ministry alone. Remember at one point he sent his disciples out into the countryside? Remember also that he sent them out two by two? Not alone, but together! And then on Maundy Thursday, after they had eaten supper in the upper room, they went to the Garden of Gethsemane, and he took some disciples with him. He said, I need you to pray with me; I need you for support. Ministry happens when we receive support and give support to other people.

My Struggle as a Woman to Find Support

Women in ministry, like men in ministry, need support. Sometimes they find support much more difficult to obtain. When we ask people in ministry, "Where does your basic support come from?" they usually answer, "My spouse" or "My family." Unless they are women. Many women in ministry have neither spouse nor family and therefore cannot find support from these traditional sources. The sources of support we can assume for most men we cannot assume for most women.

Often women in ministry have unusual difficulty finding support. I did. Even in the beginning nobody encouraged me to go into the ministry. When I suggested I would, nobody said I ought to. In those days everybody assumed somebody in my family must have been in ministry for me to think up such an absurd idea as going to seminary. But it was not true. And I cannot think of one person from those years who told me, "Lynne, it's a good idea." I knew inside that my mother and father were for me; I felt a great deal of support from them through all my years of growing up. But I never heard words of support from anyone in my local church community. Never.

I attended Drew Theological School, in Madison, New Jersey, basically because I wanted to be near New York City. I did not know any women who were graduates of Drew or of any other seminary. The only pastors I had known were men. Right at the outset of seminary I had an experience that made me feel as if women in seminary were not ordinary. About three weeks into the first semester a newspaper reporter met with the six women who were enrolled at Drew at the time. The reporter asked each of us what she wanted to do when she graduated. Evidently, women in seminary were preparing for something unusual. I did not disappoint her. I told her I would like to be a missionary in the South Sea islands. I fantasized lying on the beach and sharing the scriptures with those who walked by.

Another Drew experience was related to the Seminary Singers. After we women had attended two or three rehearsals we were told, "Your voices don't fit with the men's." It was such a disappointment not to fit again, especially for me, because music was a highlight in my life.

After a brief pastoral experience in New Jersey, following graduation, I returned to Maine. I served two small churches for three years. Then my husband (I was married at the time) and I moved to New Orleans, he to pursue a graduate degree in clinical psychology and I to enter a clinical pastoral education program at Southern Baptist Hospital. What a marvelous institution that is, but prior to my arrival the program had never included a woman, never included a United Methodist, and never included a Yankee! This was another don't-quite-fit situation.

After my experience in the South I moved back to Maine, to Aroostook County, to serve as pastor of small churches. I continued to be a "first" woman minister in many areas, struggling many times for support, especially from my peers, as well as with the decision whether or not to ask for a change of appointment. During an initial session with a Pastor-Parish Relations Committee, the only concern the committee members had was with my sex: "What has happened because you are a woman? Do you think a woman can minister? We don't know if we are ready for a woman. We're not sure the people can relate to someone without two small children." At the end of the session I found myself hoping the committee would say "No," that they did not want me. This was not the case, however, and as a result, we survived a number of months together.

But now the time had come when I decided I needed to answer some questions for myself about ministry in my life. My basic concern was whether there was a place for me, a single woman in ministry. Can I fit into the parish, especially in Maine? As I searched for an answer I kept asking, "Who is supporting *me*? Who is working on my behalf? Is there anyone who cares about me and the kind of ministry I do?" I would have to discover the answers to these questions myself.

I tried. During the next few years I attended graduate school, served on the staff of a retreat center, and supervised a seminary field-education program. All the while I searched myself and other people for clear directions. Finally, I felt, in being open to the Holy Spirit, that I was being guided back to parish ministry. In 1979 I returned to serve two small churches on the Maine coast. From there I was called to serve as district superintendent in the southern district of the Maine Conference.

The Church Must Decide to Support

Where I am going from this moment on in ministry, where other women are going in their ministry is up to all church members—women and men. Whether our journeys as women in ministry even begin is up to all of us who are the church.

Support does not just happen; a decision must be made to make it happen. Jesus consciously chose twelve people and taught them to support. When he needed support these disciples gave it to him. We have the same kind of responsibility for one another. Although denominations differ in scripture and in procedures of placement and of appointment in ministry, support begins with the willingness to give it.

Consider a woman who is called to ministry. Let us assume she is a member of the local congregation. First of all, for her to begin her journey toward ministry she must feel confirmed in herself. She needs to have a strong ego, but she also has to be able to reach out to other people to find confirmation. Ministry cannot emerge without support. Each step in this woman's preparation must be carefully planned and discussed with appropriate persons. All along the way she has to be able to talk about her future expectations, to raise questions, to share her concerns, and to find the support she needs to confirm her in her calling.

Throughout this process it is particularly important for those in authority to relate supportively to women candidates. If this does not happen, the supporting process breaks down almost before it begins. As a woman faces ministerial systems in the initial stages of her journey, her entire future is being shaped. Those of us who make up the system need to ask ourselves some important questions.

When those of us who hold positions of authority in the church know a woman is interested in ministry, we need to ask ourselves bluntly, "Do I care about this person? How do I come across to her? Do I answer her, respond to her, or do I simply say, 'Well, yes, it's too early to tell. Just take our time'?" Many women are very sensitive, especially if the person in authority is male. It is easy to project and for a woman to pick up the fact that we are not interested in her. We do not want her to bother us because there are good men out there just waiting. At least that is the way it may seem.

Then, as a woman continues her journey, the support of peers takes on increasing significance. In Maine this kind of support is taken seriously, and a special program has been established for those in the first five years of ministry. There are also district clergy groups in the United Methodist Church, as well as cooperative parish clergy groups. The Maine Conference Women's Clergy Group, the State of Maine Ecumenical Women's Group, the New England Ecumenical Women's Group, and the Portland Area Ecumenical Women's Group—*all* these groups are necessary for the support of women in ministry in that area. All the meeting dates are known and are priorities for women in that denomination.

A System of Support

When this kind of *system* of support is developed a woman in ministry finds a network of support available to her. Let me share how this system works. First, any woman in ministry in the Maine United Methodist Conference cannot be rejected because of her sex. When a woman becomes a minister in this conference, like a male clergyperson, she *must* always be appointed to a charge. Persons in authority know this is so; so do persons in local churches; and women know it as well. When the support is built into the system it is mandated.

Women need such a support system, because even with it they must still struggle against old mind-sets to earn their credibility. Women in Maine who serve churches as United Methodists range in age from the late twenties to the late seventies. Their experience stretches from first year in a parish to forty-second year in a parish. Many serve small congregations. But regardless of size of church, they face old mind-sets. For example, all too often a woman officiating at a funeral or speaking at a graduation or baccalaureate encounters a man who says something like, "Oh, there is going to be a *woman* minister speaking; I don't know about that." Generally, the outcome is, "Wow! I didn't believe it, but it *is* really true; you are good like they said." But the women have to weather that kind of experience and many like it again and again.

There is another issue clergywomen in particular face, especially younger women in ministry: Sometimes older women, laywomen in the church are jealous of the woman pastor. The problem is one of authority; these laywomen have dominated that church for years, so they look at the new pastor and wonder, "What can she do? At her age, what can she know?" I think this was part of my problem in the church I served that did not want a woman pastor. This sort of problem generally straightens itself out once the woman pastor has been at work for a while. It takes time, however, and can be a costly struggle for that woman pastor to go through.

It seems like there are always unresolved struggles for her to face up to. One of these struggles has to do with language. Because many women pastors are feminists, the continued use of sexist language in congregations and among peers is of great concern to them. Another frustration is the lack of systematic advocacy for women in some denominations. For example, I know women graduates of Baptist and of United Presbyterian seminaries who are waiting, searching, knocking on doors, sending resumes, and getting nowhere. Of course, some denominations simply do not have the needed power to reach down and affect grass-roots acceptance. Even the United Methodist Church, which has that kind of power, has a long way to go.

I believe some people in the church system are reluctant to give women clergy opportunities until they have "done enough time." I am not advocating that a woman who has been in ministry for only a year should be advanced to serve the same kind of church or be in the same kind of position as a man who has had ten years of experience. But we do need to examine our prejudices and ask honestly whether their cumulative effect blocks the advancement of women in ministry from the bottom of the career ladder, because many talented women still seem to be in the least demanding situations year after year.

I sometimes think men hesitate to advance a woman to a position of leadership in the church for fear men will lose that position for good. I know how that kind of fear works. In one of the churches I served we attempted to be inclusive in the ushering system. For years, only men had been ushers. I felt it would be good for women and children and youth to usher also. But the men came to me on a special occasion and said, "Lynne, if we can't continue to usher, then there is no place left for us in church." I was sensitive to this point and understood what they were saying. We do need to be concerned about whom change threatens. Always.

Women's Natural Gifts in Ministry

In conclusion I want to point up the gifts I see women bringing to small congregations. First, I see women unique in their natural caring for *all* people in a congregation. Sometimes men in ministry tend to relate more to those in a congregation who are professional than to the others. Women generally relate to everyone in the same caring way.

Second, women in ministry have a desire to serve collegially. To them, the pulpit is not sacred, nor the administrative board, nor the nominations committee; they do not have to dominate. They *share* leadership in the Sunday morning service; they encourage others to lead in church committees.

Third, women are hardworking.

Fourth, women have a natural sensitivity and an unusual ability to reconcile.

Fifth, women relate easily to people in the church and in the community, because people relate easily to women as persons. People are intrigued by women in ministry. This provides an advantage—an opportunity to share deeply with people. Often such sharing brings forth feelings of support and respect.

Sixth, many women in ministry are involved in social concern, social justice, human rights, and outreach. Some people in the congregation say, "Wouldn't you know it; it's just like a woman to reach out to all those people—to work with the needy and underprivileged." Now that's the kind of significant statement we all need to take a look at!

Seventh, women pastors are likely to encourage *lay* leadership, particularly the leadership of women in local churches. For many years denominations have worked hard to find ways to enable more lay leadership in the local church. A woman pastor symbolizes the broadening of ministry, opening possibilities to men becoming involved as well.

But for a woman to have the opportunity to be effective in ministry, she needs someone who will open the doors. She needs support. This support must come from the congregation she pastors, to be sure, but it must begin in the congregation where she begins. It must come as well from those who are in authority positions in her denomination. It must come from her peers. Whoever you are, it must come from you.

6

Judicatory Interventions Can Help Small Congregations

Loren B. Mead

HISTORY SHAPES WHAT happens when judicatories intervene in congregations of any kind, especially in small congregations. That history is carried in the experiences members of the congregation have had over the years with their judicatory, experiences that form patterns, that often rule over whatever the current judicatory executives might hope, plan, or expect when they enter a congregation.

Often such executives are upset when they are met with hostility even before they begin sharing their hopes. They are equally upset when met with total passivity from people who do not even know what the executives have to offer.

Every executive intervention bears the weight of that congregation's cumulative experience of itself and of its relationships with previous executives. If the congregation has felt put down, neurotically dependent, manipulated by previous executives, they are likely to expect the same from the current one, no matter how different that person's plans and intentions may be.

Moreover, every intervention occurs within relationships that have a history. Executives and congregations may re-

[77]

member negative experiences from the past and bring these feelings to the new intervention.

Usual Interventions

Over the years there are several points at which interaction between a small congregation and a judicatory typically takes place. The judicatory usually considers these matters of normal (often annual) business. But for the congregation, the emotional content is often of a new intervention into its life.

One of the most normal interventions focuses on the budget. The parish treasurer tells the executives, "We have done all we can, and the budget is still three thousand dollars short. We have to increase our asking from the presbytery (diocese, conference, etc.)." The executives' response is something like, "But the prebytery budget is already over-committed for next year because of our new priorities around theological education. Besides, isn't it time you really began to close the gap?"

Anyone who has been part of such a conversation could complete it. The point is that with the best of intentions, the executives and the members of the congregation regularly find themselves as adversaries around shrinking resources, with all the potential for hard feelings that this evokes. The congregation tends to feel as though they have come again, hat in hand, to the back door to ask for a handout, that they have been scolded for being wasteful, spendthrifts, or lazy. The judicatory ends up feeling as if it has been a miserly Lady Bountiful and as if money would not solve the problem anyway.

The second intervention—a request to make a benevolence contribution (or assessment) for the judicatory budget—quickly follows the first. Everybody pretends not to know the reality that what the congregation is here "contributing" to the judicatory budget has just been granted as a subsidy ten minutes before.

A third intervention occurs when a national or judicatory emphasis or program comes along that is considered important by the judicatory. It is rarely stated that continuing subsidy of the congregation depends on the congregation's "taking its part" in such a program, but the thought does cross peoples' minds.

A fourth intervention occurs if the congregation needs to borrow money for any purpose. Most judicatory guidelines require careful consultation of some sort, usually by the same people who establish what the subsidy will be.

Still another intervention occurs when a pastor leaves and a new one is selected. Small congregations learn that their freedom of choice is relatively limited and that the voice of the judicatory is heard in the land.

The Pattern of the Interventions

In almost all these interventions the primary agenda being served belongs to the judicatory. The primary power is that of the judicatory. The authority (financial, religious, or what have you) tends to be in the hands of the judicatory, regardless of the polity.

Meetings are called at the convenience of the judicatory committee on the turf of the judicatory. Time available to the congregation is limited, often severely, by the judicatory committee's (or staff's) need to cover a lot of other territory. Many times congregations are called into group meetings (convocations, associations, etc.) so that the staff can say what has to be done once rather than many times. I agree; the staff time available for judicatory intervention in congregations *is* severely limited. Very severely limited. There are a lot of congregations for them to cover. And what needs to be done takes considerable time in each congregation if it is to be done well.

My experience is that *adequately* helping a congregation through the period of the vacant pulpit takes from six to ten

[79]

full days of staff time. Most judicatory staffs can give little more than one evening, three or four telephone calls, and perhaps a final one-hour conference. That kind of staffing pattern guarantees second-rate (if not third-rate) interventions. The chance for an effective intervention is wiped out by the lack of time to do it well. Often the kind of intervention that results is so limited that I wonder if it should even be tried.

Shortage of time also contributes to the fact that few judicatories have ways for a *congregation's* questions or needs to be *heard*, much less responded to. Judicatory committees usually meet with more agenda than can be managed. A genuine question from a congregation may not find the appropriate agenda space for six months, by which time the response may not be useful.

The overall pattern is a church welfare system with small congregations as dependent clients, who feel to get any help at all they have to jump through procedural hoops that often seem demeaning. Harassed, overworked staffers, when they can give any help at all, are so rushed that they give little more than a bit of advice. The system is set up with the best of intentions, but the pattern of interaction reinforces dependency (neurotic, not existential) and results in lack of self-worth on the part of the congregations.

Developing a Strategy for Healthier Interventions

First, I want to ask: Do you the judicatory *want* to deal with the dependency power issue? To mess with the present system is costly. The system does *work*. It is not too comfortable, and it leads to a lot of anger and kicking back and forth. But *changing* the system will involve some pain. For everybody.

Here are the kinds of questions that need to be answered by the judicatory: Are you willing to have congregations build coalitions around *their,* the congregations', interests? Are you willing to have a bunch of churches get together to work up their own agenda and advocate it? Can you resist trying to sneak in a staffer under the guise of being the "coordinator"? Are you willing to let go and not try to control? You know congregations. If they are given some freedom to respond, sometimes they are going to say, "No," not "Yes." The present system is set up so that they always say, "Yes," even when they do not intend to. Are you willing to take the gaff of dealing with people who are going to be straight with you and say, "No"? It is almost easier to deal with people who lie and say, "Yes," and do no.

Are you willing to lose some control? If you start intervening in a different way, you are not going to be able to control things, you are not going to be able to call the outcome.

Are you willing to allow congregations to enter into contractual relations, where they can fire the person who is helping them? (That is the one thing they cannot do to the judicatory person, who is part of the dependent system.) There is absolutely no way a judicatory executive can consult with a congregation. There is no way because he or she has power in the system. What I am saying is that the executive *cannot* consult. Some staffers for an executive *can* consult, but even this is not easy. The executive may be clear about the role of consultant he or she wants to fill, but in the situation he or she is dealing with other people who have learned different expectations.

I believe executives need to think about the difference between consulting and leading, and that is a painful thing to do. Many executives, under the guise of consultants, have been hiding the fact that they are slightly nervous about leading. If an executive wants better intervention, she or he must be prepared to accept a leadership role and allow others to do the consulting, and not play games. That is the price for the executive.

The congregation has some questions to answer too. A lot of time and energy are required in order to enter into a different kind of relationship with the judicatory. You as a congregation have to work at it. You have to sit down and have meetings. Sometimes long meetings. Do you want to do that? Do you want to take the responsibility or would you rather go on blaming people for what is wrong? It is much easier to play "Ain't it awful!" Do you *know* how to do it differently? You may not know how to play a role of equality in relationship to your judicatory. You may not know how to be adults; you may have been trained so well to be childish that you do not know how to act any other way. There will be hard work, reinforcing, and practicing.

And are you as pastors willing to take the flak, because things will not go nice and easy? The present system, bad as it is in some parts, generally works. Budgets *do* get made. Decisions *are* ground out. And in the final analysis, the responsibility is covered. Doing it a new way will make waves with committees, with lay officers, with judicatory groups that have grown accustomed to the dependent structures. They may resist responsibility.

Some Needed Changes

If we all say yes to enough of these questions to want to try a different intervention pattern, some new staffing patterns will probably be necessary. I can suggest a few examples.

Robert Freyer, in the Presbytery of Louisville, has nine people on his staff. Most of them are pastors of small churches. He pays them for one, two, or three days a week. What used to be called a subsidy to the congregation is now paying for staff who have some skills in small churches. He is providing resources to congregations that way—it is different. It is hard, it is complicated, and it is not easy to do your teamwork in this style. But that is one other pattern.

Another pattern is one that Bishop Arthur E. Walmsley and Carol Kann, both of the Episcopal Diocese of Connecticut, are trying. In each judicatory they are developing a group of people who are trained to be consultants to congregations. These groups receive fees from the congregations, but the judicatory provides the training for them.

There are nondenominational agencies who can also provide intervention help; individuals, like Douglas Walrath, in Strong, Maine; the Center for Parish Development, in Naperville, Illinois; the Alban Institute and the Mid-Atlantic Training Committee, in the Washington area. There are skilled consultants listed in directories of such organizations as the Association for Creative Change.

If we *do* want better interventions and are willing to pay the costs, we must move to a different style of intervening in congregations. We need to find the congregation's change points, not the *judicatory* change points. We need to learn about the times in the life of the congregation when change is possible. Then we have to gear up with skills to be effective. There are at least three congregation change points:

One is a crisis. Any time a crisis exists in a congregation, there is a chance that change can occur and that an intervention will be helpful.

A second change point is the change of pastors. Whenever there is a change of pastors, an entry from the judicatory is welcome and sometimes very helpful.

A third opportunity is when a congregation requests help. These are the instances I can think of. Judicatories *ought not to mess* with congregations unless they are asked for help *or* get permission to come in. And the congregation ought always to be able to say, "No."

Let me elaborate on an important change point. The one holy and predictable change point (somehow this sounds almost familiar, does it not?) is when there is a change of pastoral leadership. *Every* time there is a change of pastoral

[83]

leadership the congregation is open to help. Unfortunately, the help given is usually of low quality. The usual entry is for the judicatory to provide a set of mimeographed sheets outlining the steps required and to tell the church, "Go out and hire somebody, and let us know who it is." Sometimes there is a bit more, but not much.

A well-planned entry recognizes that this opportune time to help significantly comes along once every two, four, five, or ten years in the life of every congregation. It is predictable. One can prepare to be effective. The opportunity is going to recur. If the judicatory is ready with real resources, it can help a church take *giant* steps of growth. Pastoral transition is a key developmental movement in the life of a congregation.

There are four developmental *tasks* that *every* congregation must perform if it is going to enter into a *healthy* relationship with a new pastor (United Methodists, pay attention to this, because by and large, United Methodists listen to this less than anybody else!). These tasks *can* be done if the judicatory is ready. Whether they take one week or six years to complete does not matter. But if a pastor is to have a new kind of pastorate in a small church, they can clear the way.

First, the congregation has to come to terms with the past. The ghosts of past clergy must be laid to rest. People have to complete their grief work to be ready to work with somebody else.

The second thing they can do is to deal with the shifts in lay power that occur with every change of pastors. Frequently, in the calling systems, for example, the person who is head of the pulpit or search committee within two years becomes the chief lay officer of the congregation. But this is only one of many shifts in power that usually occur within a congregation. For example, people who have been active with one pastor decide that they want to move to the back pew with the new one. It is important to help a congregation through these shifts in leadership.

The third developmental task is to rediscover the denomination. Congregations, whatever their denomination, become very congregational when a pastor is in full-time residence. They take their understanding of the denomination from what the pastor tells them. During this period of pastor changing they have a chance to meet the denomination in a new way. They find out what the denomination's values are, they meet other pastors from the denomination. They find out whether the denomination really cares about its congregations and its pastors. They learn whether or not the denomination can *help*.

The fourth developmental task is to help the congregation get a clear fix on its identity. One of the things that happens when there is a pastoral change in a small congregation is that the congregation may *also* have to be deciding to change the character of the way the pastorate is done. It may be facing closure or going to a part-time pastor or yoked relationship. That is the time the congregation needs even more help. It is scary to lose your pastor and to have to face the fact that things are going to be different. By and large, judicatories I know are very poor in helping congregations with that.[1]

Conclusion

In developing a strategy for intervening helpfully in small congregations, judicatories have an enormous opportunity in the predictable crisis points. These are "teachable moments"—moments when the congregation's needing help can be matched by the judicatory's making available skilled resource persons and methods. The biggest question for the development of strategic interventions is whether the judicatory can give up its need to establish programs, promote activities that meet its needs to develop the ability to respond to the needs of the congregations—the needs of the congregations *as seen by the congregations*. Judicatories that are committed to that will be building up skills and learning to listen to congregations; they will not be generating projects and programs. They will leave congregations alone until they are asked for help. And they will learn all they can about predictable change points and crises in congregations, so they will be ready when the call comes. They will be willing to commit significant amounts of staff time or consultant energy for significant interventions and not fritter away those human resources by trying to cover every base all the time with the same amount of energy.

What do we need to know more about? We need to know more about how creative judicatories are learning to make available significant chunks of staff time through new staffing patterns. We need to know what kinds of small-church coalitions are developing and what happens to them when they choose to do things different from what the judicatory wants. We need to know how such coalitions are born and how they grow and die. We need to know new standards of "success" for the small church (such churches will probably always be "failures" by the ordinary standards of denominational success—numbers, dollars, buildings).

Finally, I want to raise questions about the battle cry of the small-church movement. Everybody tells me, "Small is beautiful." I have heard this until I am sick of it. It has gotten to the place that I feel I am a heretic even to question its obvious truth.

Small is beautiful? Not always! In the church, small often means broke. Small means defeated. Small means overextended. Small means other people make your decisions for you. Small means put down, beat up, hurt.

I know the reality behind "Small is beautiful," and I affirm much of it. But I just want us to get away from the sickly, romantic hogwash that goes under that banner. There can be beauty in smallness, but the overwhelming experience in the church is that frequently it is not beautiful.

I want to affirm something more important. While small is *not* always beautiful, it is enough. Small is enough.

It is enough for keeping on. It is enough for faithfulness. It takes only two or three, Jesus said. Most small churches have at least a dozen or two. Small is enough for holding lives and families together and for making a contribution to a community. It is enough for breaking bread and sharing wine, for wrestling with the scriptures, for calling one another to new life. It is enough for praying, for following Jesus. What else do we need?

7

Small Churches Can Be Powerful

Theodore H. Erickson

THE ATTENTION THAT has been given to the small church during the past seven or eight years has made it clear that small churches are qualitatively as well as quantitatively different from large churches.[1] The small church is increasingly seen as a distinctive segment of denominational life, possessing unique strengths and expressing the need for determining its own destiny. If the trend within mainline Protestantism is toward more diversification within denominations,[2] the small church surely emerges as a specific type that requires sustained attention, regardless of denomination.

Changing Patterns of Power

While less attention has been paid to the changing character of judicatory bodies, there appears to be an observable drift toward increased power and authority at the regional level of denominational organization. Whether as a true judicatory, in the Presbyterian sense, or as a connectional unit, in the Methodist sense, or even as an associational body, in the free church tradition, regional organizations seem to be increasingly active as policy and program entities, absorbing some of the power traditionally exercised by strong churches, on the one hand, and by national denominational agencies, on the other.

One might expect that an increasingly powerful judicatory might be of greater assistance to the increasingly well-defined needs of small churches. But I do not believe this to be the case. The reason for this lies in the shifting patterns of power.

As the judicatory assumes more power it tends to perceive the churches in its jurisdiction as subunits of itself. Within this context the smaller or weaker churches are perceived as increasingly dependent, contributing fewer resources per unit than their larger counterparts, and also as demanding more attention per capita than the judicatory can comfortably provide. Meanwhile, the smaller churches, resentful of their dependent status, recognize the need to enhance their own identities by increasing their own measure of power.

The question, therefore, is not how the judicatory can effectively help the small church, but rather how the small church can effectively assert itself vis-à-vis the judicatory in order to develop fully its inherent potential.

One of the more striking observations to emerge from the United Church Board for Homeland Ministries' small-church project several years ago was that achieving power is an essential ingredient for church revitalization.[3] The original title of the project was Small Church Empowerment. Early on, the word empowerment was dropped because it was thought to be too presumptuous. On reflection, however, clearly the question of power was central both to the problems that were encountered and to the manner in which the project was pursued.

The central fact of life for most small churches is lack of power. Small churches lack power in their denominational settings and in their community settings. As one listens to the testimony of small-church leaders, lack of power, lack of ability to do what needs to be done emerges as the crying need.

Small churches today face three basic questions: Is achievement of power a legitimate goal? Is achievement of power a recognized and accepted goal? Is achievement of power a realistic goal?

Legitimate Power

1. Is achievement of power a legitimate goal? Christian attitudes toward power are deeply ambivalent. Power is of God. The faithful are blessed with the power of the Spirit. We as Christians affirm the power of prayer and we are moved by the power of scripture. The church as Christ's body incorporates and directs the power of Christ's ministry.

But we are suspicious of corporate power—perhaps with good reason. We are schooled in humility. We confine our experience of power to the sanctuary or to the inner reaches of the soul. We keep our power under a basket. We may claim to be enlightened, but we rarely claim to be empowered.

The good reason for maintaining modesty with regard to corporate power is that true believers have been known to go astray. Holy crusades, ancient or modern, can become self-serving mockeries of the causes they espouse. Mere righteousness can become a substitute for mature faithfulness.

But the gospel, we must all admit, was not proclaimed in order that it be confined. It was proclaimed to free the world from bondage, both spiritual and temporal. The truth may, from time to time, be hidden, but it is not secret. It is to be lived, personally and corporately, as an ever-present witness to God's sovereignty.

Power originates in the experience of worship. The size of the congregation does not determine the degree of religious experience that worship generates. But the social power of the congregation does have an effect on the degree to which religious experience can be translated into productive activity. The tension between perceiving the power of the Spirit and witnessing to this power in concrete, everyday situations is at the heart of every church's dilemma. The dilemma is particularly acute and most appropriate in the small church. A large church may achieve some success, some status, some change in social direction. Its members may be lulled into believing that they exercise some power. Whether or not actual power is related to potential power is another question. The experience of achieving is enough to reduce the tension.

In the small church, however, the tension persists. Its members may succumb to resignation, but deep inside the reality of powerlessness remains. Faithfulness must find an outlet, must be witnessed to if it is genuine.

Achieving the power to witness corporately is not only legitimate, it is essential for Christian life. When the social structure of achieving such power inhibits the church's witness, it is time to examine that structure and to discover ways by which the barriers can be broken.

Small-church Empowerment

2. *Is achievement of power a recognized and accepted goal* within small churches? The experience of powerlessness, especially generation after generation, leads to low expectations. The church exists in a network of relationships, more important, relationships within the larger community and within its denomination. Low expectations are communicated in a thousand ways, overt and subtle. "I don't have much to offer you," they say, "and so I don't expect much from you." Is this the gospel? Is this the resurrection faith?

If a church lacks sufficient members, financial resources,

leadership, and relationships to express its religious experience, it may not be able to recognize and accept the need to achieve power without changing its relationships within its community and its denomination. Changing its relationships often requires sustained outside intervention. This simply means that somebody must take responsibility to help the small church out of the hole.

The Protestant tradition of church independence fosters resistance to outside intervention. If every believer is a priest, who needs bishops? But as Protestants, we tend to emphasize our priesthood at the expense of our catholicity. Christian responsibility extends to all believers as well as to all people.

The larger church has a responsibility to help churches achieve power. And churches that are in need have a responsibility to ask for help. Relationships between the larger church and the local church need not be hierarchical. A fixed hierarchy, on the one hand, can and often does contribute to maintaining real isolation among churches while espousing formal interrelationships. A tradition of mutual responsibility, on the other hand, can contribute to real interrelationship in the face of formal autonomy.

The first step toward achieving power is for the local church to reach out for help. This first step immediately changes the social situation. The United Church small-church project referred to earlier began by introducing a special category of ministry: the intervening agent. The primary task of the agent, whose overall work is described in various reports, was *not* to raise immediately the question of power, but rather to listen systematically (sometimes called research) and through listening and feedback to become part of the church's power structure.

Every church has a power structure, an informal group who must approve new directions. In small churches the power structure may be weak or it may be virtually intractable. In any case, the internal power structure is usually part of the barrier to the achievement of greater social power. It is the product of long experience of powerlessness, and until it is reoriented to achieving social power, it will remain a barrier.

One should not be led to the quick conclusion that popular notions of participatory democracy can replace entrenched power structures. The achievement of social power is the result of wise and effective leadership. The task is to develop a *leadership* structure in the place of a power structure, to move informal power into a formal arena of discussion and decision making. In order for this transformation to take place the real experiences of the members must be voiced. Leaders are those persons who can translate needs and experiences into action. The job of the intervening agent is to stimulate the expression of experiences and through this expression to discover and nurture leadership.

Thus the process of recognizing and accepting the goals of power achievement within the small church is reflexive. It is rooted in experience—the experience of the power of the gospel and the experience of frustration in adequately exercising this power. Out of the many experiences of members, a common experience emerges. Out of the common experience, new possibilities suggest themselves. Out of the perception of new possibilities, new leadership or a reorientation of old leadership emerges. Active leadership, in turn, engenders new experiences among the church members.

Of course, the word emerges is too passive. At every step the intervening agent plays an active, if only a supportive or guiding role. The agent becomes part of the power structure on behalf of but not as part of the new leadership structure. The agent also becomes an inside-outsider, a specialized participant in the life of the church who has an eye clearly on the goal: the achievement of social power by the people involved.

Intervening agents usually define their roles if not as judicatory representatives, then as consultants. The word consultant may imply more detachment than is required for real change. Self-defined consultants may limit themselves to providing resources, program ideas, drops of distilled wisdom. These are not enough. What is required is refined political sense, skillful friendship, measured involvement.

The network of primary relationships that exists in the small church creates a highly volatile political context. In the large church secondary relationships may be useful in diffusing the effects of an intruder. In the small church the politics are intense; resistance can coalesce rapidly and expulsion can take place before it is recognized.

The mark of the church's acceptance of a goal is a formal, written covenant, forged out of experience and expectation. Ironically, the primary group character of the small church enhances its ability to covenant. Membership in a small church constitutes a sort of informal, interpersonal covenant. Entrance and exit are highly visible. Loyalty is a pervasive expectation. The covenant is an open declaration of loyalty, a shared intention, the pronouncement of intentions that transcend the immediate perceived reality.

Covenanted intentions are more than dreams; they are realistic projections in a given historical context. The written covenant constitutes the first action toward the realization of the church's power.

A Realistic Goal for the Small Church

3. *Is achievement of power a realistic goal* for a small congregation? So much for theory, you may say. So much for specialized intervening agents. Can small churches achieve power through everyday denominational resources? The answer is yes . . . if. If by "everyday" one presumes sympathetic and skilled judicatory personnel who are not trapped in modes of traditional behavior. The methodology

of the small-church project has been translated into denominational activity in several locations throughout the United Church of Christ. In these locations traditional assumptions and denominational power structures have been challenged. Perhaps the most intensive work of this project has been carried on in the Penn Northeast Conference of the United Church of Christ. A conference staffer was assigned "to help our congregations develop new forms of working together with other churches (denominationally and ecumenically) and with other groups toward the fulfillment of Christ's mission." The assignment resulted in the establishment of the Local Church in Life and Mission Project, in January 1977. The project was conducted with small churches of long standing in light of four principles: (1) the changing geography of the community, (2) the increasing importance of national and regional levels of society, (3) the horizontal and vertical dimensions of community, and (4) maintenance and task functions in work with groups.[4] Groups of eight to twelve churches were identified, and the staffer began work with each congregation on a systematic, phased schedule. In time, area mission councils were formed. At first, these councils represented an overlay of ecclesiastical organization, competing with traditional associations. Then the conference acted to phase out associations and replace them with area mission councils. The conference staffer became staff to the resultant councils. Within the councils a sense of mutual caring developed among pastors who had felt isolated and, yes, powerless.

The councils became new and quite real arenas of church life, experienced most immediately by the pastors and the conference leadership. The councils also became a source of growing influence in the life of the conference; whereas the small churches had experienced isolation and the associations had reflected the anomalism of these churches, the councils, by virtue of imbuing the churches with a new sense of direction, reflected a new potency in the conference. That emerging base of power has yet to manifest itself fully in the lives of the churches. Five years is a beginning. Several decades of this kind of work may change the face of Protestantism in America.

Just as a formal covenant expresses new intentions *within* the small church, so a covenant can express new relationships and new intentions *among* small churches.[5] The interchurch covenant is a declaration of identity in the face of traditional judicatory assumptions. It is essential that the new clusters or associations of small churches themselves define the geographical extent and functional dimensions of the covenant. A covenant, by nature, cannot be imposed; its reality depends on the expressed will of its participants. Bureaucratically defined clusters of churches may serve only to increase the sense of dependency and frustration that must be overcome.

Empowering small churches is legitimate and possible. To empower requires dedicated people who are willing to intervene and challenge the status quo. Small churches, a lingering "concern" of ecclesiastical bureaucracies for generations, can and must assert themselves. If it is the case that two thirds of the churches are small and that one third of the members belong to small churches, clearly we are dealing with a healthy but oppressed minority of Christian people whose experience of spiritual power is frustrated by their structural lack of ability to exercise this power. They may potentially constitute the most important force in Protestantism. They need new leadership, and in order to generate new leadership they need new visions and leaders who can open the windows to these visions.

A judicatory, if it is to be helpful in encouraging the achievement of power for small churches, must admit openly the inherent tension between its own nature and the unique needs of its small churches. The judicatory must stimulate and make room for the growth of new relationships within and among its small churches. The judicatory must revise its expectation of success for small churches, emphasizing the quality of interchurch relationships and the exercise of social power instead of numerical growth and financial contribution. The successful judicatory can create a climate within which the small church can reach its potential. A wise judicatory understands that through enhancing the power of the small church, it increases its own capacity to serve faithfully the wider church.

The road to power for most small churches is not necessarily to grow numerically, but to grow associationally through establishing new relationships with other churches and community organizations. It is to extend the experience of spiritual power to the temporal realm and in so doing to discover the need for even greater spiritual power. It is to develop leadership with a vision of society that integrates the life of the church with the life of the community. This has been the heritage of the small church—a heritage that is rapidly becoming extinct. With determination, political skill, and unswerving vision that heritage can be reclaimed.

Notes

Introduction

1. Jackson W. Carroll, ed., *Small Churches Are Beautiful* (San Francisco: Harper & Row, 1977).
2. David R. Ray, *Small Churches Are the Right Size* (New York: The Pilgrim Press, 1982).
3. Carl S. Dudley, *Making the Small Church Effective* (Nashville: Abingdon Press, 1978).
4. William H. Willimon and Robert L. Wilson, *Preaching and Worship in the Small Church* (Nashville: Abingdon Press, 1980).

1. Possibilities for Small Churches Today

1. *Rural Sociology*, Vol. 35, No. 3 (September 1970).
2. Douglas A. Walrath, "Social Change and Local Churches: 1951-75," in Dean R. Hoge and David A. Roozen, *Understanding Church Growth and Decline, 1950-1978* (New York: The Pilgrim Press, 1979).
3. See the 1978 Gallup poll report "The Unchurched Americans."
4. Loren Mead in Moira Mathieson, *The Shepherds of the Delectable Mountains* (Cincinnati: Forward Movement Publications, 1979), pp. 106-7.
5. Willard Gaylin, *Feelings* (New York: Harper & Row, 1979).

2. Worship in the Small Congregation

1. Dom Gregory Dix, *The Shape of the Liturgy* (New York: Seabury Press, 1982). Dix notes that the old Roman basilica of Saints John and Paul still presents the exterior facade of the third-century palace of the Senator Byzantius with its windows filled in;

on the roof is "still the fourth-century tiling, laid on when he gave it to be adapted for the new public way of worship."

2. Peter G. Cobb, *The Study of Liturgy,* edited by Jones, Wainwright, and Arnold (London: SPCK, 1978), p. 474.

3. Emile Mâle, *The Early Churches of Rome* (London: ET Ernest Benn Ltd., 1960), p. 45.

4. Recollected from a lecture at the Notre Dame Pastoral Liturgy Conference, at Notre Dame University, June 1981.

5. See Gottfried Deelen, *Cross Currents,* Vol. 30, No. 4. See also Edward Schillebeeckx, *Ministry: Leadership in the Community of Jesus Christ* (New York: Crossroad Publishing Co., 1981), and J.B. Libanio, *Experiences with the Base Ecclesial Communities in Brazil,* LADOC, bimonthly publication of the Latin America Documentation, Lima, Peru.

6. Cf. *Liturgy Committee Handbook: A Nine-Week Study Guide,* The Liturgical Conference, 810 Rhode Island Avenue, N.E., Washington, DC 20018.

3. The Art of Pastoring a Small Congregation

1. For an expansion of these assumptions, see Carl S. Dudley, *Making the Small Church Effective* (Nashville: Abingdon Press, 1978).

2. For a particularly insightful discussion of this assumption, see Urban T. Holmes, III, *The Priest in Community* (New York: Seabury Press, 1978).

6. Judicatory Interventions Can Help Small Congregations

1. "Signs of the Times" (1983), Alban Institute, Mount St. Alban, Washington, DC 20016.

7. Small Churches Can Be Powerful

1. See chapters by Jackson Carroll and Douglas A. Walrath in Jackson Carroll, ed., *Small Churches Are Beautiful* (San Francisco: Harper & Row, 1977).

2. William McKinney, "The Moral Majority, the Immoral

Minority and the Embattled Middle," *New Conversation*, Vol. 6, No. 2 (Fall 1981).

3. David Brown, Robert Haskins, and William Swisher, "Small Church Project, Final Report," June 1977. Theodore Erickson, "Small by Design," 1977.

4. William Swisher, Report: Local Church Project, 1977-81.

5. Theodore Erickson, "From Process to Covenant," *Christian Ministry*, July 1977.